GINO LEINEWEBER

HEMINGWAY
HOW IT ALL BEGAN

CHILDHOOD AND YOUTH IN MICHIGAN

VERLAG EXPEDITIONEN

2014 LIT Verlag Expeditionen GmbH
© Gino Leineweber
Hemingway – how it all began
Translation: Terry McDonagh and Dalia Staponkute
1. Editon 2014
Cover: Manfred Kubowsky, Birgitta Sjöblom
ISBN: 978-3-943863-31-4

In memory
of my Father

NOTES AND ACKNOWLEDGEMENTS

I am delighted that the English edition of Ernest Hemingway's biography – his childhood and early youth as I see it - is now available. When I first visited Michigan in 2008, I discovered that Hemingway spent a lot of time in these places during his childhood and early youth. He began to write there and celebrated his first wedding in the small village of Horton Bay.

The connection between the place and the great author caught my attention and deepened my interest in his biography. When I startet reading books and articles written about Hemingway in German language, I realized that there is very little told about that pivotal part of his carrier as writer. I followed his path to places where he spent time as a child and a young man and wrote about it in his stories. This way I enriched my knowledge and understanding about Ernest Hemingway as human being and writer.

Investing my time and energy in the learning process about life of this great writer has been very rewarding indeed. I was lucky to meet wonderful people who were so crucial to my research and who helped me in any way they could.

I would like to express my special thanks to James Vol Fox and Bob (Robert) Metzger from Horton Bay; the Director of Petoskey Museum and a writer, Michael Federspiel; a journalist Liz (Elizabeth) Edwards of *Traverse Magazine*.

The sources that I used are indicated in the text – or in footnotes. All quotes from Hemingway's letters were taken from *Hemingway - Selected Letters 1917 - 1961*, by Carlos Baker.

My apologies, if I have inadvertently overlooked some important source.

Gino Leineweber
May 2014

To become acquainted with Hemingway and to get to know how and why he became a gifted author, it is necessary to explore his childhood and youth. To concentrate only on his exceptional daredevil deep-sea-fishing exploits, African safaris and his passion for boxing, is a superficial exercise and non-productive.

As to fully grasp the source and strength of Hemingway's literary gifts one must trace him back to Windemere on Lake Walloon in North Michigan. Those who confine him to Cuba, Key West in Florida, even the civil war in Spain as the most important stations in his life, miss out on the one place that had the greatest influence on his creative life.

And to truly understand the growth of literary qualities in the young Ernest Hemingway, it is important to lay aside tales of his legendary, obsessive drinking; his macho womanizing or his love of boxing and bullfighting. One must experience him in Horton Bay or Petoskey where he could be seen on excursion to lakes and creeks with his friend Bill, or in a hammock, reading a book. He could be seen swimming in a lake on warm summer days, feeling breezes through the spruces as he went barefoot through the wood, rowing out on a lake in the evening sun, wandering on hills or fishing for trout in Horton Creek. Here lies the root, source and strength of his literary vocation.

In her book, *Hemingway in Michigan*, Hemingway biographer, Constance Cappel compared him to a "migratory bird" that returned each summer to spent his vacation "Up in Michigan".[1]

It was here that he discovered and nurtured his writing vocation – a calling that was all the greater for these experiences as a young man. It was here that Hemingway gathered himself, created an independent personality, learned to fish, hunt, drink and meet girls. It was here where he learned to focus and take his writing seriously.

Hemingway grew up in a relatively puritanical home. His father, Dr. Clarence Edmond Hemingway, known as Ed, was a physician in Oak Park, a suburb of Chicago. Today, the Hemingway house on 339 N. Oak Park is home to The Ernest Hemingway Foundation and open to visitors. Another Hemingway home, from 1906 and also in Oak Park, is now in private hands. In 1896, Dr. Clarence Hemingway married Grace Hall, a woman of artistic disposition from a wealthy Chicago family who had wished to become an opera singer. Ed was a sporty, outdoor man who enjoyed fishing and hunting, whereas Grace's interests lay more in Chicago society and artistic pursuits.

Hemingway had four sisters and was his parents' only son until his sixteenth year, when, as the last child, his brother Lester was born. Ernest, the second child, did not have a good relationship with his parents for whom *right and wrong* was clearly defined and insisted upon – any deviation was severely punished. Card games and dancing were frowned upon and Sunday church attendance was duty bound for all family members. The boy grew into a powerful and energetic young man constantly striving to escape the choking provincial shackles of his home, determined to write and not to accept the world as it was.

In autumn 1917, the time had come for Ernest Hemingway, born on the twenty-first of July 1899, to leave home. He withstood his parents wish for him to go to college after high school. Instead, his uncle and father's brother, Tyler, intervened securing him a post as a reporter with *The Kansas City Star*.

America was drawn into The First World War and Earnest volunteered. When a colleague at the *Star* drew his attention to The Red Cross Ambulance Corps, he applied and was accepted. Towards the end of 1918, with his friend, Carl Edgar and two companions he left Kansas, once again setting out for a fishing holiday in Michigan. Here he received a telegram informing him that he was to set sail for Europe from New York on the eights of May.

The young Hemingway was confronted with war and in this warlike situation, he found his place and recognition. As Second Lieutenant in the ambulance service, he was proud to be photographed in his decorated US Army officer's uniform. However, it would appear that being *just* an ambulance corps officer was not enough for his public image, as could be seen from photos where he'd removed his Red Cross badge from his uniform.

In 1918, he crossed the Atlantic in a French liner named after Chicago, his hometown. In Northern Italy at the foot of the Dolomites he was deployed as an ambulance driver with the task of transporting the wounded from the hillsides to the field hospitals down below.

He even volunteered to take cigarettes and chocolate by bicycle twice daily to soldiers on the Front. On one of these occasions a soldier was killed and he and several others seriously injured when a hand grenade exploded in their midst. Later Hemingway was decorated with the Silver Medal for Bravery by the Italian Government. Included in his certificate of bravery was, among other things:

*Ernest Miller Hemingway... responsible for carrying sundries (articles of comfort) to the Italian troops engaged in combat, gave proof of courage and self-sacrifice. Gravely wounded ... with an admirable spirit of brotherhood before taking care of himself, he rendered generous assistance to the Italian soldiers more seriously wounded by the same explosion and did not allow himself to be carried elsewhere until after they had been evacuated.*[2]

On the sixteenth of June in 1918, in a letter to his family from his sick bed, Hemingway wrote:

*The 227 wounds I got from the trench mortar didn't hurt a bit at the time, only my feet felt like I had rubber boots full of water on. Hot water. And my knee cap was acting queer. The machine gun bullet just felt like a sharp smack on my leg with an icy snow ball. However it spilled me. But I got up again and got my wounded into the dug out. I kind of collapsed at the dug out.*

On his return to the United States, Hemingway visited his much-loved Michigan where he had spent so many carefree vacations – from birth he had spent every summer there.

The State Michigan is surrounded by four of the five Great Lakes that lie between the USA and Canada: Lake Erie, Lake Huron, Lake Michigan and Lake Superior, the world's largest freshwater lake. The name Michigan is derived from the Indian word, *Mishigami,* and roughly means, great lake – and this is no exaggeration. This term Great Lakes State is, indeed, true because more than a half of the State consists not only of the Great Lakes, but also of numerous smaller ones as well. No resident of this State must travel more than about six miles to get to a lake. In addition, particular to Michigan is an area of dry land consisting of two parts: the Upper Peninsula and the Lower Peninsula.

The main occupational activities in the northern part of the Lower Peninsula as well as in Upper Peninsula were tree felling, fur trading and fishing. These practices came to an end at the turn of the twentieth century. Since then the area lives mainly from tourism. While the signs of mass tourism cannot be fully ignored – as for example on Makinac Island – serious damage to the landscape is not evident. Tourism here is mainly of an individual nature and leaves little or non lasting damage.

Michigan is distinguished by the largest number of National Parks in the United States. However, its greatest fame comes from the city of Detroit – the hub of the car industry. This is situated in the extreme south east corner of the Lower Peninsula, whereas tracing

Hemingway leads northwest and to the Upper Peninsula.

From 1898, the Hemingway family spent their vacations – firstly with their first daughter Marceline and later with their six children – captivated by the magic of Northern Michigan among undulating hills, lakes and forests. Here they would remain undisturbed for the duration of the school vacation. Dr. Hemingway could not always be with the family due to the pressures of work and need to earn a living.

In their first visit, they were so taken by the beauty of the countryside around Walloon Lake – then called Bear Lake –that they looked around for land on which they could build a holiday home. Henry Bacon, who was later called "Grandpa Bacon" by the children, provided them with what they were after: 4,000 square meters of land and lake where they could spend their vacation. They built a simple, structurally sound cottage with a large fireplace in the living room. As the years went by, the cottage was gradually extended. Water was pumped by hand from their own spring well. An oil lamp gave light for reading and piano playing. The south west veranda provided a good view of the lake and parents could keep an eye on their children. A toilet was built in the little pine forest at the back of the house.

There was a little sandy strand and in the blue water of the lake, they would swim and wash their clothes. The house was surrounded by birch, cedar, oak and beech. Grace baptized it "Windemere" after a lake in England. Life was lived in and around water. It was a constant source of fun and entertainment. Dr. Hemingway spent a lot of time with his children, teaching them swimming including lifesaving drills – he drilled them in these techniques and even organized swimming competitions to ensure that the children could compete in their disciplines.

Over the years the family had ships of all kinds from rowing boats and canoes to their first motorboat in 1910. In a different context, Marjorie Bump, a friend and playmate of the children, had the following to say:

*Dr. Hemingway was a wonderful man who was easy to love. He had eyes like the softest cashmere, with kindness buried inn their depths. One stormy night, he had to be tough and scold us after our nighttime lark of going out canoeing on Walloon Lake without permission. Even then, his eyes were expressively kind and tender though his strong disapproval reminded us that we had not been safe.[3]*

Furthermore, under their father's guidance, the children got to know all about fishing. Dozens of family photos with trout, pike and perch, bear graphic witness to the success of his instruction.

Shooting was an integral part of the Hemingway family vacations as well. Clay pigeon shooting was central to Sunday afternoon fixtures. And they didn't shoot just for fun – hunting was, also, a leisure activity. However, Dr. Hemingway's clear instructions to his children were that no animal was to be killed that could not be eaten later.

Windemere was open house to guests and special festivities. Family members, including grandparents, came for extended visits. There was a barbecue with friends on the Fourth of July, American Independence Day, and, in 1911, their daughter Carol was born in Windemere.

The fun and freedom the children enjoyed at Windemere was in no way curtailed by their having to contribute to duties and responsibilities involved in the daily running and upkeep of the house. Despite the doubtless idyllic vacations, Hemingway in his book, *Earnest Hemingway on Writing*, had nothing positive to report on his childhood:

*Question: What is the best early training for a writer?*
*Hemingway: An unhappy childhood.[4]*

He felt lost and not understood in this family dynamic consisting of a domineering mother and weak father. But he was enriched, could forget the world and be happy in the forests and lakes of Michigan, where he could fish and hunt beyond the bounds of his restricted life in the city of Chicago.

His experiences in Michigan greatly influenced him and became part of his writing. In his younger years – 1916/17 – Hemingway wrote his first three short stories which were published in the school journal, *Tabula*. It is said that a writer can only write what he experiences, and the young Hemingway began to shape stories about people and places in Michigan he knew and understood.

In, *Judgment of Manitou* (he uses the Ottawa Indian word Manitou that means God), it fits the picture when he writes on nature and violence: here conflict between two men, near the Canadian border, ends in death. The two trappers Dick and Pierre are the main characters in this short story. Pierre has become suspicious of Dick thinking that he has taken his lost wallet. So he sets a snare trap for Dick when he goes out to check his bear trap. Dick is soon caught and he is left hanging from a tree, to meet his fate of being eaten by timber wolves. Pierre soon realizes that it was a red squirrel that stole his wallet. He rushes out to find what's left of Dick and he himself then is caught by Dick's bear trap to face the "Judgment of Manitou".

The second story, *The Matter of Color*, is more an anecdote than a short story. There's neither rising action nor dramatic effect, and it is suggested it should be read aloud to capture the accent, slang or message of the story. The story deals with a match between the two boxers, a white, Montana Dan Morgan, and a black, Joe Gans. Dan has hurting his strong punching hand before the match. Therefor he is unable to use it. The two go along with the fight. Dan before, paid a large Swede, to hit Joe over the head from behind a curtain next to the ring. But the Swede ends up hitting Dan and knocking him out. He hit the wrong man because he was colorblind.

In this third story, *Sepi Jingan*, there is contact, for the first time, with an actual person, the Indian, Billy Tabeshaw, who would later also appear in his Book *The Nick Adams Stories*. The inclusion of real existent people would be a feature of Hemingway's stories from then on. *Sepi Jingan* likes to draw on stories from the Indians tradition. It is the name of a dog who saved Billy's life. Billy tells the story of a Indian named Paul Black Bird, who killed the game warden that got caught him spear fishing illegally. The game warden was Billy's cousin, so Billy sought revenge and tracked Paul with his faithful dog, Sepi Jingan. After two years, on the Fourth of July, Paul Black Bird was found dead on the train tracks. The people thought that he had gotten drunk and was killed by a train, labeled by events that allegedly occurred. But Billy knows better. On that very day he and his dog had run into Paul. The problem was, Paul saw them first and knocked Billy to the ground with a pike-pole. While Paul toyed with his prey, Sepi Jingan crawled toward him from behind and attacked and killed Paul. Billy then put Paul on the railroad tracks that caused people to conclude that Paul had lain down on the tracks in a drunken stupor.

In these three stories, Hemingway established a style and pattern that we find again and again in his later work. All three have a surprising ending and Michigan as a backdrop. In two of them Indians are portrayed as figures who are protagonists. Even in his younger years he sought out places that influenced his writing most, and he never changed this pattern in the course of his lifetime. The experiences, the surroundings and happenings in Michigan find expression and can be recognized in much of Hemmingway's work. As against that, Hemingway's years spent in his main home in Oak Park, Chicago, where hardly mentioned.

These influences are especially noticeable in the *Nick Adams Stories*. Here we have a collection of short stories incorporating Hemingway's *alter ego*, Nick Adams, and which were published in various editions at different times.

The book, as it is, was first published in 1972. In addition to previously published texts, it also contains work that had been unpublished at that time. The publisher sorted the stories, written between 1922 and 1933, chronologically and divided them into five categories.

The first category, *The Northern Forests*, describes the landscape and living conditions in Michigan. Hemingway's ability to describe a landscape is evident from the beginning of the prologue.

*'Of the place he had been a boy he had written well enough. As well as he could then.' That thought a dying writer in an early version of "The Snows of Kilimanjaro". The writer of course was Hemingway. The place was Michigan of his boyhood summers, where he remembered himself as Nick Adams. As well as he could write then was very well indeed.* [5]

To seek out places described in this book leads to the area around Petoskey in the north west of the Lower Michigan Peninsula and to Seney in the Upper Peninsula. The focal point is Horton Bay – a name that already appears at the beginning of the *Nick Adams Stories*. Horton Bay and Horton Creek – the little river that flows round Horton Bay – are referred to in the fifth story, *The Indians Moved Away*.

Prior to that, Petoskey and its surroundings are described in the story. Whereas Horton Bay is tiny, the focus is on Petoskey, the main town in the district Emmet County. It is situated in the north western part of the Lower Peninsula, and which, with Cheboygan, forms the most northerly point.

The Hemingway family had their cottage on a site near Walloon

Lake. In 1905, this was extended to Longfield Farm to the other side of the lake. The Hemingway land was cared for and worked by a farmer in their absence and by the family during vacations. When Dr. Hemingway acquired the forty acres, it was his wish that his children should learn and appreciate the value of honest physical work as well as the farm providing them with food during summer vacation. In 1917 a further twenty acres were added and local farmer, Warren Sumner, employed. In this summer of 1917, when he was eighteen years old, Ernest and Sumner spent most of the time renovating the old farmhouse. He cut hay and built an ice house. Sumner took ice blocks from the lake in winter and stored them in the ice house to provide refrigeration for food and cool drinks for the Hemingway family in summer. Ernest had fulfilled his father's wish that his son got to know the value of physical labor – at least for a time.

What his father didn't like was that Ernest devoted a lot of time for reading literature. He read all the classics – especially English authors who were in abundance in the local libraries. An old nanny of Hemingway's recounted Dr. Hemingway's orders to take the books from Ernest, with the words: *Each evening I'd search his cabin and take away all the books. When I'd tuck him in, he'd say good night, as sweet as could be, then in the morning I'd find books stuffed under the mattress, in the pillowcase, everywhere. He read all the time – and books way beyond his years.*[6] Another person who, occasionally, helped out at Windemere, recalls: *We saw a lot of Ernie when he was a kid, but later on, not so much. He went off in the woods and he read a lot. He was sort of a loner. Always took this pup tent of his and went fishing somewhere alone.*[7]

For the Hemingway children, vacation times could be described as being idyllic, even if Dr. Hemingway insisted on having them around him when felling trees or gathering fruit. There were duties and chores – such as going for milk to Grandpa Bacon's Farm – but these did nothing take from the idyllic state; not even when, at the beginning of their stay, they had to help out with repair work and improvements in house and garden. The journey from Oak Park to Michigan, at the time, would have been strenuous but that would have been more than compensated for by the joyful anticipation of time ahead.

In relation to the north west of Michigan, the home town Chicago is situated on the other side of the Lake Michigan. The family journey, loaded with cases and boxes, would begin at Chicago River Dock, usually on the steamer "SS Manitou." Their luggage was then unloaded at Harbor Springs in Michigan and brought to the local station from where they travelled with the "Grand Rapids & Indiana Railway" that connected Harbor Springs and Petoskey which was eleven miles away. It is here in this city, Petoskey, that Hemingway set his first novel, *The Torrents of Spring*.

After they'd completed the journey to Petoskey via the dune landscape that surrounded the bay, they'd to change for Bourbon station which was only one block away, but which took them direct to Walloon Lake Village from where they could, finally, get to Windemere by ship. Grand Rapids & Indiana Station is still intact and being renovated. Today it is used as a business and shopping center. Bourbon, on the other hand, is no more — it is now a car park.

The strenuous journey over, Ernest and his family immersed themselves in a natural world they knew and understood and one that was so different from the pressures of the so-called civilized world they had come from. This, however, did not mean that they were allowed to ignore hygiene or appear unwashed and untidy at table in Windemere. But the countryside and natural world where they spent those wonderful summers allowed them access to nature in its purest form. This is old Indian territory. The Ojibwa Indians of Michigan, also lived in Canada, Wisconsin and Minnesota, north and south of Lake Huron and Lake Michigan. They lived from fishing, hunting and harvesting wild water rice. Their lands were unsuitable for agriculture and were, thus, spurned by the white settlers. The Ojibwa's people, with their extended families and sub-tribes, have survived and are to be found in various reservations in Canada, as well as in the United States in North Dakota, Michigan, Montana, Minnesota and Wisconsin.

In the first story in the *Nick Adams* book, Hemingway relates his childhood experiences in which Indians are portrayed as active participants. For example, in the story, *Indian Camp*, when Nick's father, the doctor, is called to assist at the birth of a child, he is collected by two Indians in a rowing boat. Nick is allowed to travel with them. This short story contains brutality, misery, birth and death – even hidden racism, as some would say. The story was first published in Paris in 1924 in a slim thirty-two page book with the title, *in our time*. The lower case was deliberate. Indian Camp was the first publication of a Nick Adams story. There is a dramatic moment in the book when Nick's father performs a caesarean section, without anesthesia, on the Indian woman, with a sick husband lying in the upper bunk above her. Nick held a bowl while three women and a man held the woman down. After the birth, the husband was found with his throat cut from ear to ear – he'd committed suicide during the birth. To Nick's question, *why,* his father replied: *I don't know, Nick. He couldn't stand things I guess.* But what was it, really, that he could not endure? Was it the screams of his wife or "white" doctor's disregard? For when Nick asked his father to try and stop the woman screaming, his response was cold and direct: *I don't have an anesthetic with me,* and: *But her screams are not important. I don't hear them because they are not important.* After this statement, Hemingway wrote: *The husband in the upper bunk rolled over against the wall.*

*Indian Camp*, as the stories is named, is most certainly the Indian settlement behind Windemere. All of the Indians who lived there worked as bark-peelers for the big tree-felling companies. When the mills closed, the base camp closed with it. Together with Nick's father and Nick, there was Nick's uncle, George who went to the Indian Camp. Ernest himself did have an uncle, also named

George, who lived in Boyne City and who, after he had read this story claimed there was not a bit of the truth in it. Anyway, this proves nothing because it is not clear whether the uncle was around at the time of the incident. It is a fact though that Dr. Hemmingway had often helped out when a doctor was needed and he had assisted at births.

In the story, the father-son relationship is handled delicately. When Nick's father discovered the dead husband, he regretted having brought his son with him. He apologized to him, but it was too late – Nick had seen everything.

In this story, the apparent low esteem, in which the white Americans hold the Indians, is not immediately comprehensible. The words, in which the screams of the pregnant Indian woman were ignored, could be written down to the "doctor conducting himself in a professional manner."

But seeing Indians as a kind of "second class" did exist and is graphically described in the story, *Ten Indians*. After the Fourth of July festivities were over, Nick travelled home with the parents of friends and all along the way, their driver, Joe Garner, had to stop and drag Indians, lying on the road, to put them aside:

*"That's nine of them," Joe said, "just between here and the edge of the town."*

*"Them Indians," said Mrs. Garner.*

The Hemingway holiday home and Walloon Lake was somewhat west of and a few miles distant from Horton Bay. The lumber camp, close by, was known locally as the Indian Camp because most of the inhabitants were the Indians who'd provided the background for the two aforementioned stories. Reading into the *Indian Camp* story, father and son seem to get on well enough. Although the father regretted having taken his young son with him when the Indian committed suicide at the birth, it would appear it was his son's wish to be allowed to actively participate in his father's life.

Indeed Ernest had always praised his father for having shown him everything he could, as well as having taught him things a father ought to teach his son.

As against that, Ernest and his mother did not have a good relationship. Even when he was an eighteen-year-old reporter with *The Kansas City Star*, she made him justify, in a letter, his reasons for not going to Sunday church.

He wrote to her then that he had to work till one after midnight and sometimes later on Saturdays. Sunday was the only day where he could catch up on his sleep, and she should not worry about him not being a good Christian. In his own words:

*I am just as much as ever and pray every night and believe just as hard so cheer up! Just because I'm a cheerful Christian ought not to bother you.*

But in the same letter, he made it perfectly clear that he could speak his mind:

*Now mother I got awfully angry when I read what you wrote about Carl (Edgar) and Bill (Smith). I wanted to write immediately and say everything I thot (thought). But I waited I got all cooled off. But never having met Carl and knowing Bill only superficially you were mighty unjust. Carl.. is the most sincere and real Christian I have ever known and he has had a better influence on me than any one I have ever known. ... I have never asked Bill what church he goes to because that doesn't matter. We both believe in God and Jesus Christ and have hopes for a hereafter and creeds don't matter.*

Bill – William Smith Jr. – the person in question, was a good friend from their vacation times in Michigan. He and his sister Kate (Katherine) spent the summer with their aunt. She, Kate, would, later, become the wife of the American author, John Dos Passos, who wrote, among other things, *Manhattan Transfer*. We meet her with Carl Edgar (also mentioned in the letter) in Hemingway's short story, *Summer People*. So, Ernest got to know Carl, whom he'd named, Odgar, through Bill and Kate. Odgar, who'd, later, shared house with Hemingway in Kansas City, was madly in love with Kate. It is described in *Summer People*, but it is Hemingway's *alter ego*, Nick, who has a sexual relationship with Kate:

*Down the roads through the trees he could see the white of the Bean house on its piles over the water. He did not want to go down to the dock. Everybody was down there swimming. He did not want Kate with Odgar around. He could see the car on the road beside the warehouse. Odgar and Kate where down there. Odgar with that fried-fish look in his eye every time he looked at Kate. Didn't Odgar know anything? Kate wouldn't never marry him...*

Yet later Nick met Kate and Odgar and, on the way home, a late-night rendezvous was arranged:

*The car, in low gear, moved steadily up through the orchard. Kate put up her lips to Nick's ear.*

*"In about an hour, Wemedge," she said. Nick pressed his thigh hard against hers. The car circled at the top of the hill above the orchard and stopped in front of the house.*

*"Aunty is asleep. We've got to be quiet," Kate said.*

They said their goodbyes but, later, Nick and Kate meet in the forest and make love. This does not, however, correspond with the true story. There is no evidence that Butstein, as Hemingway called Kate in life and in the story, had a sexual relationship with Wemege (Nick).

A letter from September, thirtieth in 1920 to Grace Quinlan, a girl from Petoskey, Ernest was befriended with, talks of a night on the booze during which Kate and Ernest enter a Catholic church and light a candle. It would appear that this was the first time that Hemingway, raised as a strict Protestant, had entered a Catholic church. This incident is worth mentioning because, at a later date, Hemingway converted to Catholicism out of love for his second wife. On his visit to the church, he wrote: *Then Kate and I went to the catholic church and I prayed for all the things I want and won't ever got and we came out in a very fine mood and very shortly after to reward me the Lord sent me adventure with a touch of romance.*

Having read this, one would not know what to think. In the same letter in which Hemingway mentions a romantic experience, he writes that he composed a poem for Grace, the receiver of the letter, on the way home. He considered Grace, six years his junior, as his sister. It would appear that this is a smokescreen to cover up his true feelings for her – his interest and care are a lot more than one would expect from a brother and sister relationship. In a letter dated on the twenty-first of August in 1921, in which he invites her – also Marge (Marjorie Bump), another girl from Petoskey – to his forthcoming wedding, he cautiously suggests it could all have been very different. *Know how you feel about my being too young to be married. Felt exactly the same....*

He no longer had these feelings and this was because of his future bride, Hadley. Grace had been too young for marriage – even five years younger than the other girl Marjorie. But what if Grace had not been so young? His compliments in his letters to her would suggest that his feelings for her went far beyond brotherly affection.

Kate, with whom he's experienced a touch of romance, died tragically in a motor accident in 1947 when her husband, John Dos Passos blinded by the sun, collided with a truck that had come half-way across the road. Kate was flung through the windscreen and died instantly. Dos Passos lost his right eye but survived.

W indemere was the place where, in younger years, he'd spent important and impressionable times during his summer vacations, but as grew older, he began to spend more time in the company of Kate and her brother in Horton Bay, a small place nearby, that attracted visitors in summer time. Away from the family, Ernest was free to behave like a typical teenager, trying to impress girls, hanging out with friends or using his storytelling talent to exaggerate tales of hunting and fishing or, indeed, happenings in the far-off city of Chicago.

The place Horton Bay, named after a man called Horton, is not longer, with one exception, to find on signposts, because it is part of Bay that stands for Bay Township, which is easy to find when somebody leaves the road from Charlevoix and crosses a small bridge over Horton Creek. That little river is referred to, for the first time, in the story, *The Indians Move Away*.

The creek meanders round the place – a magical, picture-book landscape of little rapids weaving round mounds of sand, mossy stones and decaying tree remains leaving a vital and vibrant impression in its path. Overgrown meadows and dense woodland present pictures known from Hemingway's tales. For the observer, his depiction of the natural beauty of the north of Michigan is just as true today as it was in Hemingway's stories.

This is how one should try to imagine the little rivers and creeks in question. Horton Creek is not only preserved in the short stories mentioned, but remains as a template for other creeks in other Hemingway stories. This small river stands for and symbolizes Ernest's childhood experiences – and fishing – especially trout fishing which was not always allowed.

In two passages in the story, *The Last Good Country*, Nick fished for trout without permission. His sister asked him first:

*"Did you get many, Nickie?"*

*"I got twenty-six."*

*"Are they good ones?"*

*"Just the size they want for the dinners."*

*"Oh, Nickie, I wish you wouldn't sell them."*

*"She gives me a Dollar a pound."* Nick Adams said...

*"I'll go through the woods down to the inn beyond the point and sell her the trout,"* he told his sister. *"She ordered them for dinners tonight. Right now they want more trout dinners than chicken dinners. I don't know why. The trout are in good shape. I gutted them and they are wrapped in cheesecloth and they'll be cool and fresh..."*

When crossing the bridge over Horton Bay Creek, after a while a few houses coming in view – this is Horton Bay. In the story *Up in Michigan* Hemingway describes the place, sometimes spelling it differently: *Hortons Bay, the town, was only five houses on the main road between Boyne City and Charlevoix. There was the general store and post office with a high false front and maybe a wagon hitched out in front, Smith's house, Stroud's house, Dillworth's house, Horton's house and Van Hoosen's house. The houses were in a big grove of elm trees and the road was very sandy. There was farming country and timber each way up the road. Up the road a ways was the Methodist church and down the road the other direction was the township school. The blacksmith shop was painted red and faced the school.*

Coming into Horton Bay, today, one can see a small business, the Horton Bay General Store, built in 1876. It is still the center of the business and social life in the township. Hemingway describes it not only in his short story *Up in Michigan*; it also seems to be the outline for Mr. Packard's Store in *The Last Good Country*. In the shop you will find pictures and memorabilia from and to Hemingway.

And even much more so in the next house, the Red Fox Inn, that Hemingway referred to Horton's house. In front of the hotel, there are Hemingway signs and a display case with memorabilia, pictures, clothing, accessories, books and baseball caps with inscriptions: "Horton Bay" and "Hemingway". There's also a collection of signs. Among them a plaque, stating that the Red Fox Inn was built as a boarding house for loggers in 1878, as well as being a hotel acquired by James Wixham Fox in 1910 and taken over by his son, Vollie in 1919. In that year, they restored the house and it became an excellent venue for summer guests. Otherwise most of the plaques and signs refer to Hemingway. He had given the hotel a present of a helmet from The First World War, complete with a bullet hole. A sign with the suggestion below said that this was what he was referring to in the *Three Stories and Ten Poems*, published in Paris in 1923, as well as in the story, *Up in Michigan*. In addition, there's a plaque that proudly states: "Hemingway slept here".

This is true, and he, probably, slept there more than once. There is evidence that he slept there prior to his first marriage, which he celebrated in the village. When open the hotel door, having climbed back up the five steps to the porch of the Red Fox Inn, and entering the room one can see shelves laden down with card racks, cabinets, chairs and books. A wooden table in the middle of the room is full of books. On the left at a former reception desk, there are books, pamphlets, pictures, mementos – everything bears but one name: "Hemingway". The Red Fox Inn is a shrine to Hemingway.

It is run today by James Vol Hartwell, the grandson of Vollie and Lizza Fox, who is only too pleased to reveal the connection his family and the hotel had to the famous writer. Perhaps it's not all true, but that's not so important. According to James, his grandfather had taught Hemingway fishing, but this can't really be true since, in the story, *Fathers and Sons,* Hemingway had expressly praised the father of his *alter ego* Nick for having taught him how to fish. True is, however, that Vollie was fishing with him.

When you go down to the Bay from the Red Fox Inn on the opposite side of the road, you realize that much is, naturally, not in the condition it had been when Hemingway described it. Nevertheless, the two Houses of Dilworth resort are still intact on the left hand side of Lake Street. Here Hemingway had the "Wedding Breakfast" of his first marriage. It is mentioned in the stories, *Summer People* and *Up in Michigan.*

Both houses are still in the possession of the Dilworth family, albeit the ex-husband of a granddaughter. The first of the two houses, Pinehurst, is the original residence of the Dilworths. It and a forge were built in 1910. Later the boarding house was built next door, which is still in business. Today, it is called Shangri-La, as, indeed it was described by Hemingway: the sign above the door says, Shangra La. The forge is also still there, no longer in its original state but as a replica. James Dilworth was a blacksmith.

Apart from roads that are no longer the sand paths in the stories, you can still get a clear impression of the place described by Hemingway. At the end of Lake Street is the dock, mentioned in some texts. Still intact, on the other side of the bay, is the old boat house, seen as background to a photo of the young Hemingway taken in 1919 after he'd returned from The First World War, wounded and decorated as a hero – and also proudly displaying three freshly caught trouts in his hand.

The boathouse is built on the place where the Horton Creek flows into the Horton Bay. Among other things the bay is referred to in *The End of Something.* One can be taken on and experience the course of a boat-trip described by Hemingway in this story. It begins with a flashback to the closure of the great mill which had been, to a great extent, the main source of income for the people of Horton Bay:

*In the old days Horton Bay was a lumbering town. No one who lived in it was out of sound of the big saws in the mill by the lake. Then one year there were no more logs to make lumber. The lumber schooners came into the bay and were loaded with the cut of the mill that stood stacked in the yard. All the piles of lumber were carried away. The big mill building had all its machinery that was removable taken out and hoisted on board one of the schooners by the man who had worked in the mill. The schooner moved out of the bay toward the open lake, carrying the two great saws, the traveling carriage that hurled the logs against the revolving, circular saws and all the rollers, wheels, belts, and iron piled on a hull-deep load of lumber. Its open hold covered with canvas and lashed tight, the sails of the schooner filled and it moved out into the open lake, carrying with it anything that had made the mill a mill and Horton Bay a town.*

With this, a story begins with Nick and Marjorie rowing along by the old disused mill. It's the year of that trout-photo, where we see Hemingway as a handsome, bright and happy young man. Despite his traumatic war experiences, he appears interested, dynamic and strong – a direct contrast and light years away from the picture of the sick, corpulent, depressive and untidy Hemingway of later years. It is sad and moving when you compare them.

However, he is not as bright and breezy on the boat trip as he appears in that picture of him. Marjorie and he have been fishing and, afterwards, they land to have a picnic near the boathouse on the other side of the bay. Nick is in bad mood and when Marjorie asks him what happened to him, he tells her the truth. *It isn't fun anymore. Not any of it.* His remarks are rude and unambiguous – Marjorie has been crudely rejected. Later, after she returns by boat alone and disappointed, and Bill comes out of the forest – the same Bill Smith, from that summer in Michigan – he wonders if she is happy to be away. Nick confirms she is. Bill then asks if there had been *a scene*. There *hadn't been*, according to Nick. When Bill wants to know how he feels, Nick asks him to stay away.

The story is rather autobiographical. Marjorie did exist, but the incident is far from true. On the contrary, when Marjorie learned that Hemingway had used her name without her permission, she was really upset. Marjorie retold her daughter, Georgie, the whole story shortly before her death in 1987. From Georgie's book, we learn that Marjorie had always felt deeply hurt by Hemingway's portrayal of her in literature, which had nothing to do with reality:

*I felt humiliated to be the object of their pity when they read about me as the young lady to whom Nick (as Ernest) had spoken these words about our relationship: It isn't fun anymore.*[8]

In later life she avoided telling to her surrounding that she had known Hemingway at all. She was haunted by it throughout her life. She went so far as to have her middle name, Lucy and not Marjorie on her grave stone – at least she could finally be consoled. Ernest did write, once, to say "sorry." His exact words:

*Everything understood is everything forgiven.*[9]

Carlos Baker, Hemingway's authorized biographer, describes the first meeting of Hemingway and Marge in the summer of 1919 when he was twenty and she seventeen:

*Marjorie and her friend Connie Curtis had come from Petoskey to wait on tables at Mrs. Dilworth's. She was seventeen, with red hair and freckles, dimpled cheeks, and a sunny disposition.*[10]

But this is not true – even if this version of the story is to be found not only with Carlos Baker, but almost always when speculating about Marjorie and Ernest in Horton Bay. Repetition is indeed no guarantee of veracity. Tales get passed on, and people pass them on believing what they want to believe.

Marjorie Bump was born in Petoskey on twenty-fourth of August in 1901. According to her, she did not come to Horton Bay to work as a waitress and, in fact, Ernest and Marjorie, first, met in 1915 and not in 1919. Her account:

*The first time I saw Ernest Hemingway, I was walking back from Horton's Creek, where I had caught my first fish with a cane pole. Both of my hands were full of fish and I was so proud and exited that I forgot to be afraid to talk to an older boy even though I didn't even know his name. I wasn't yet fourteen as my birthday would be coming up on August 24th. During the first meeting, Ernest probably saw me as a short, young teenager with red hair, green eyes and freckles. What I saw was a tall, handsome boy with dark eyes who appeared to be about sixteen. Ernest stopped to admire my fish.*[11]

Marjorie had come to Horton Bay to visit her uncle, Professor Ernest Ohle, who had a holiday home there. At the same time, Ernest had visited his friend Bill Smith. At the end of their first meeting Hemingway made a move towards her:

*"Well, Red, I like your beautiful fish and since you're such a sport I might take you with me to troll for rainbow trouts some day at the point."*

*"Would you really, truly? You won't forget, will you?"*

*"No chance of that. I need an extra hand with the boat, and you'll do."*

Marjorie added: *Happily for me, Ernest did not forget his offer. It extended throughout my adolescent years as he often found the time to take me to fishing for rainbow trout, bass, and perch in Horton Bay.* After that, Marjorie and Ernest met regularly. Marjorie's cousin, William Ohle, describes a meal at his parent's house, which was opposite Dilworths' residence. This took place in 1917:

*Ernest... sat uncomfortably at the table speaking in monosyllables as my mother tried to keep conversation going.*[12]

But, in fact, Marjorie spent more time with Hemingway's sisters, especially Ursula, who was her age. Those who doubt these facts that Ernest and Marjorie meet in an early age – because they all come from Marjorie – need look no further than the pen of Hemingway himself, for their verification. On the sixth of December in 1917, when he was already in the army, he wrote to his parents from Kansas City:

*I got another Army thing the other day too that is great. An Army slip on sweater. Khaki wool. Marge Bump knitted it for me, and it is a peach of a sweater.*[13]

How could Hemingway have worn a "peach of a sweater" that Marjorie Bump had knitted him for the war in 1917 when, in Baker's words, Ernest first had met and a summer romance with her in 1919? This letter is not included in Hemingway's collection, edited by Carlos Baker.

Ernest and Marjorie did have a relationship. Maybe a romance. It is obvious that the fishing and boat trip in the story *The End of Something* was intended to be used as an opportunity to finish the affair of the character from Nick with the character from Marjorie on that evening. This is obvious not only from Bill's questions, but also from the subsequent story, *The Three Day Blow*, in which Bill says, "it's a good thing" that Nick finished with Marge:

*"It was the only thing to do. If you hadn't, by now you'd be back home working trying to get enough money to get married."...*

*Nick said nothing... All he knew was that he once had Marjorie and that he had lost her. She was gone and he had sent her away. That was all that mattered. He might never seen her again. Probably he never would. It was all gone, finished...*

*"If you had gone on that way we wouldn't be here now," Bill said.*

*That was true. His original plan had been to go down home and get a job. Than he had planned to stay in Charlevoix all winter so he could be near Marge. Now he did not know what he was going to do...*

*He had talked to her about how they would go to Italy together and the fun they would have. Places they would be together. It was all gone now. Something got out of him.*

From this excerpt and the further discussion it is clear that the Nick and Marge were not engaged, but had intended to marry; that

Nick had wanted to spend the winter in the city to be closer to Marge and that he didn't particularly like Marge's mother and her stepfather. Nick was confused and felt really sorry for the way he had treated Marge as can be seen from the story – *going into Town on Saturday* – where he had wanted to meet her and to improve things.

There seems to be little doubt that Marjorie's mother didn't like Ernest in reality, if you can believe Marjorie, and there seems to be reasons for not liking. It would appear that Hemmingway had seriously considered marrying Marjorie. However, it would seem that his intention had more to do with material things than with romance.

Years later, Marjorie's mother had told her that Ernest had discussed marriage with her, but she replied to the young fellow that her daughter was far too young, and that they should wait until they had graduated from college before considering an engagement or marriage. During this conversation Ernest had clearly asked Marjorie's mother if it were true that her daughter would inherit money from her grandmother; and this was confirmed... But the inheritance would only be received after the death of her grandmother. Ernest needed money for writing and had, probably, thought Marjorie could help.

Marjorie, or Marge in the *Nick Adams* stories, was just part of the Michigan idyll that Hemingway describes when writing about summers and other times spent there. The first meeting of Ernest and Marjorie is especially idyllic: creeks, fishing and an innocent girl meets an innocent boy on the road. This perfect world ended six years later when Hemingway married his first wife, Hadley, and turned his back on Michigan. From stories told by him and from between the lines it is quite clear that there had been a lot more than friendship between Marjorie and Ernest in that perfect summer and autumn of 1919. It was not just the holiday romance that it is thought to have been. The facts suggest that it was a relationship that had carried on for years, but we do not have details on the romantic aspects of their time together. We are, perhaps, left in a dilemma...

We can only speculate about the romance of 1919, but that there had been a relationship we can conclude from Ernest's conversation on the marriage with her mother. It could be asked why their relationship is reduced to a summer romance? No one has answers but the biographer Kenneth S. Lynn, has even fewer when he takes it one absurd step further: he contends that in the two stories, *The End of Something* and *The Three Day Blow*, Marjorie is the young embodiment of Hemingway's first wife, Hadley and not Marjorie from Petoskey at all.

That Lynn's insights probably missed the point can be seen from a letter of Christmas eve, 1925 which Hemingway wrote to F. Scott Fitzgerald (who at that time was working on his famous *Great Gatsby*). From the letter, it is obvious that Hadley is not intended: *The only story Hadley appears in is* Out of Season. The two stories involving Marjorie are from the time before this letter. Why Kenneth S. Lynn ignored some important facts? Perhaps it is his style to ignore the facts even when they speak against him... And Lynn's accounts of Hemingway's war experiences can also be questioned.

On the other hand, in literature, it is not always possible to ascertain what exactly initiates a story or is any driving force behind it. In Hemingway's stories there are actual happenings, landscapes and places in Michigan that, under other circumstances, would correspond with the facts, but a consideration of the facts is not what it's about. It is not about the authenticity of Hemmingway's descriptions; instead, it concerns itself with the literary concept and the subject matter of his stories.

A writer sees the world from his perspective. The readers are allowed access, but his and readers' world won't necessarily correspond. Everyone has and shapes his or her own inner world. The feelings and emotions described by Hemingway are so intense that it would be difficult to ascribe them to the young Ernest as actual happenings – they must be seen as figments of imagination in his story. The gentleness and sensitivity seen in quiet moments and his need for affection are as much in evidence in Hemingway's literary work.

Whether Marjorie or Hadley, who appear in both stories, were real or not is theoretical and unimportant for Hemingway's writing, or for his opinion on states of mind. The facts about Marjorie are indisputable – whether or not she is the character in the stories is open to dispute.

However, in both stories we read about young people going through their experience of a relationship in the knowledge that it could end in marriage. In this case it does not. This was the world of the young Hemingway preserved in his writing, which allows us to see into his life and in the landscape of Michigan a century later.

The landscape, experienced by Hemingway or other people at the beginning of the twentieth century has, naturally, been conditioned and altered by time, but the changes have not been as dramatic as in other parts, given the timeframe of almost one hundred years.

At least, in Horton Bay one does not have the impression of a lost or another world. The stories of Hemingway and his Nick Adams are still recognizable, but the earlier Michigan is nowhere to be seen. At the turn of the twentieth century, the countryside was changed dramatically when the old forests were exhausted and deforestation began to spread in earnest in. Although Hemingway did not experience this destruction around him, he says he was sickened by the ruined American landscape and terribly upset by the loss of the native ancient forests and pristine rivers.

The actual state of the North Michigan landscape of the earlier time can be reconstructed from Dr. Hemingway's diary sketches and photos from their road trip with his wife, Grace and sons Ernest and Leicester in the summer of 1917. The whole family would usually has travelled by boat and train, but this time only their daughters travelled that way.

By car, the journey took five days. They slept in tents and fished for food and, with the roads in such a terrible condition, the journey was a real adventure. Detours added a 100 miles to the scheduled 487. They had a shovel with them to get the car going again when they got stuck. The last 31 miles from Traverse City to Walloon Lake was particularly precarious. The sand roads were so bad that they could only drive at an average of about 8 miles per hour. As well as a shovel, they had an axe with them to chop branches that had fallen across the road in places. It even became embarrassing when, under the watchful eye and wry smile of a farmer, their T Ford got so stuck, it had to be rescued by horses. On the way back they – and the car – travelled by boat.

Things are very different nowadays. The shovel and axe need not be travelling companions on a car trip to Northern Michigan any longer. But perhaps Hemingway might not have approved this, because, even then, he commented in his writing critically about the interference with nature. He wouldn't have experienced the change to its full extent. If one considers what he would have faced at the time, then it looks that he must have been exaggerating. In his complaints he is, for example, dealing with water pollution and waste, indeed, a huge topic of discussion in Chicago at the turn of the twentieth century and the solution was, as he has described, a flood relief channel. But Chicago is situated in the southwest of the big Lake Michigan whereas the area around Petoskey, where Hemingway spent his vacation in "his Michigan," is in the northeast. And he could only have known of deforestation by hearsay. But are such things not of great importance for a writer? His consternation about the changes taking place in Michigan is genuine. In 1947, he wrote to his colleague, William Faulkner:

*My own country gone. Trees cut down. Nothing left but gas stations, sub-divisions where we hunted snipe on the prairie, etc...*

His sadness about the violation of the landscape is clearly expressed in the story, *The End of Something*, when Nick and Marjorie are out rowing on Horton Bay. At the beginning of the story he bemoans the closure and disrepair of the great mill: *what makes a windmill a windmill and what makes a town a town.*

It's true that the loss of the last of the ancient forests brought change and damage to the Michigan landscape. When the trees were cut down and then the train tracks neglected, the towns died and houses, apart from a handful, fell into disrepair or got ruined altogether.

However, the changes that have taken place from Hemingway's childhood and youth to the present day have not been too drastic. If, today, you drive the road described in the story, *The Indians Moved Away*, you can see that it still is readily identifiable.

*The Petoskey road ran straight uphill from Grandpa Bacon's farm. His farm was on the end of the road. It always seemed though, that the road started at his farm and ran to Petoskey, going along the edge of the trees up the long hill, steep and sandy, to disappear in the woods where the long slope if fields stopped short against the hardwood timber...*

Grandpa Bacon was the Henry Bacon who had sold them the site for their cottage, Windemere, in 1898. The Bacons and Hemingways became good friends and prior to Hemingways buying their own farm, Henry provided them with milk, meat, butter and vegetables. It was on the Bacon farm that the Hemingway children got their first introduction to life on the land. In return, Dr. Hemingway provided the Bacons with medicinal and medical care at little or no cost, and Ernest gave Henry a tiny place in history when he included his descriptive directions to Petoskey in one of his short stories.

The road is, naturally, not in the same condition as it was when it was described by Hemingway about a hundred years ago. Even a car by today's standards, would hardly have mastered the journey without assistance. In those days, roads were unsealed. Uphill meant mastering a sandy slope. It was advisable never to travel without a shovel and axe – the axe to clear the road of fallen branches. Today, they are no longer needed. You travel up and down hills, undisturbed, rejoicing in the beauty of the surroundings from a hilltop and, as is often the case in the USA, you can travel miles and miles up and down on seemingly endless undulating roads.

And despite the fact that Hemingway might not have welcomed the changes to the landscape, he loved it just the same, as can be seen from his remark to his first wife Hadley when they were driving through Little Traverse Bay: *See all that. Talk about the beauty of the Bay of Naples! I've seen them both, and no place is more beautiful than Little Traverse in its autumn colors.* [14]

Hemingway describes a particular landscape in the story, *The Last Good Country* – a woodland area northeast of Horton Bay. But it is not only his description of the landscape that impresses – his outline of the destruction wreaked upon the forests of Michigan by people and lumberjacks is graphic. Nick and his sister discuss this while travelling together:

*They came from the hot sun of the slashing into the shade of the great trees. The slashing had run up to the top of a ridge and over and then forest began. They were walking on the brown forest floor now and it was springy and cool under their feet. There was no underbrush and the trunks of the trees rose sixty feet high before there were any branches... No sun came through as they walked... His sister put her hand in his and walked close to him.*

*"I'm not scared, Nickie. But it makes me feel very strange."*

*"Me too." Nick said. "Always."*

*"I never was in wood like these."*

*"This is all the virgin timber left around her... Don't you worry. There it's cheerful. You just enjoy this, Littless. This is god for you. This is the way forests were is left. Nobody gets in here ever."*

The *Last Good Country* is not a short story, but the beginnings of a novel that, sadly, Hemingway never completed. In sixty-three pages, he manages to build up so much tension that it almost pains considering that the story comes to an end at the heart of it. The idea for this story reaches back to his youth in 1915; to an unusual incident involving Hemingway and a heron. Around the time of his sixteenth birthday – somewhere near July, twenty-first – Hemingway managed to startle a heron and shoot it from the boat. Apparently, because a heron was missing from their collection of stuffed animals, he'd wanted to make a present of it to his father.

Ernest wrapped the heron in newspaper and hid it in his boat. Unluckily, it was discovered by the son of the local game warden, who started questioning him. Hemingway pretended he'd got the heron from an unknown man. Nevertheless, two strange men appeared at Windemere next day and asked the same questions. Ernest told his mother the true story, and she suggested he should go and hide in the Longfield farm on the other side of the lake. – It was a farm owned by the Hemingways and where they grew fruit and vegetables.

So, Ernest was not around when the two men called to the house.

In a letter to her husband, dated 30.7.1915, Ernest's mother outlined the meeting with the men like this:

*I thought them burglars or fiends of some sort. They had such a beastly, insinuating, sneering way, and would not state their business. They fired questions after questions... I said if you know so much about my business and that of my family, you don't need to give me any further impudence. This tackling a lone woman and her little children without giving you're your business or authority and asking impudent questions is not the way to behave yourselves, and just you remember it the next time.*[15]

After that visit, Grace Hemingway sent a message to Ernest to be on the lookout for a better hiding place. He took her advice but, first, went to Jim Dilworth and his wife, Liz who had a chicken grill business in Pinehurst Cottage. Still on the run from the gamekeepers, he found refuge in his uncle's summer house close to Ironton and situated on the opposite side of Lake Charlevoix. Later, on his father's advice, Ernest admitted his guilt to authorities and paid the fifteen dollar fine. Apart from the visit to his uncle's, the incident is included in the draft of the novel, *The Last Good Country*.

One of Hemingway's sisters plays a role in the novel as well – she accompanied him on that run. The real story tells that, at the time of the shooting of the heron, his sister Sanny – about ten and a half years old then – was present at the moment. However, from Hemingway's written lines in *Nick Adams Stories*, it is doubtful that the character which in the story was given a pet name, Littless, had to do with sister Sanny. Most probably it was Ursula. In the story she is described as follows:

*His sister was tanned brown and she had dark brown eyes and dark brown hair with yellow streaks in it from the sun. She and Nick loved each other and they did not love the others. They always thought of everyone else in the family as the others.*

Ursula's hair and eyes were dark brown and much would indicate that she was Nick's sister, Littless. In the *Nick Adams Stories*, there is a further indication of the special relationship shared by Hemingway and his sisters when in the story, *Fathers and Sons*, Nick omits his father's unpleasant smell.

*Nick loved his father but hated the smell of him and once when he had to wear a suit of his father's underwear that had gotten to small for his father it made him feel sick and he took it off and put it under two stones in the creek and said that he had lost it... When Nick came home... and said he lost it he was whipped for lying.*

*Afterwards he had sat inside the woodshed with the door open, his shotgun loaded and cocked, looking across at his father sitting on the screen porch reading the paper, and thought, 'I can blow him to hell. I can kill him.' Finally he felt his anger go out of him and he felt a little sick about it being the gun that his father had given him.*

And further:

*Their were only one person in the family that he liked to smell of, one sister.*

The relationship between Nick and Littless in *The Last Good Country,* exceeds what would usually be understood as a brother and sister relationship. This impression filters through the whole story which begins with Littless kissing her brother with both arms wrapped round him.

Later Nick says to her: *I'd like to kiss you* – and then the special attraction becomes more explicit in the scene where Littless sits on Nick's lap, embraces and hugs him with her head against his cheek. After some time, suddenly and abruptly Nick tells her to get off his lap with the excuse that he has to prepare a meal. She, then, asks if she can kiss him while he's taking care of the meal. The suggestion of some commentators that he was sexually aroused by the presence of his sister sitting in his lap is nowhere to be found in the story. But, from the text, one could feel that Nick was aware and concerned about this bond that went above and be-yond a normal brother, sister relationship:

*He loved his sister very much and she loved him too much. But, he*

*thought, I guess those things straighten out. At least I hope so.*
However this is not Littless's outlook on life. Her dreams about the future life are made clear at breakfast. Nick asks:

*"Did you sleep all night?"*

*"I'm still asleep. Nickie, can we stay here always?"*

*"I don't think so. You'd grow up and have to get married."*

*"I'm going to get married to you anyway. I want to be your common-law wife. I read about it in the paper."*

*"That's where you read about the Unwritten Law."*

*"Sure. I'm going to be your common-law wife under the Unwritten Law. Can't I, Nickie?"*

*"No."*

*"I will. I'll surprise you. All you have to do is to live a certain time as man and wife. I'll get them to count this time now. It's just like homesteading."*

*"I won't let you file."*

*"You can't help yourself. That's the Unwritten Law. I've thought it out lots of times. I'll get cards printed. Mrs. Nick Adams, Cross Village – common-law wife. I'll hand these out to a few people openly each year until the time's up."*

*"I don't think it would work."*

*"I've got another scheme. We'll have a couple of children while I'm a minor. Then you have to marry me under the Unwritten Law."*

*"That's not Unwritten Law."*

*"I get mixed up on it."*

*"Anyway, nobody knows yet if it works."*

*"It must," she said.*

Here again we see how the impetus comes from the younger sister – an infatuation that, most probably, went beyond what's considered normal. As the passages referred to in the story show, Nick's expectations, at the time and for the future, do not correspond with those of his younger sister, Littless.

Although, in real life Ernest Hemingway felt very close to his sister Ursula, and always spoke fondly of her, there is no further evidence of an incestuous relationship between Ernest and her or one of his other sisters at all. He was more positively disposed to his sister Sanny than he was to his oldest sister, Marceline – which was quite remarkable. Even their mother had considered Ernest and Marceline, more or less, as twins and had raised them as such. It seems the mother had tried to unite them in a special brother, sister bond. In a letter to his publisher, Charles Scribner in1949, Ernest wrote that his mother didn't succeed, and this way he clears up any misconceptions there might have been about him and his relationships with his sisters. He also complained about an article about him that appeared in the magazine, *McCalls*:

*How could this miserable McCall woman possess the gall to even think of writing about me and my family? The cheek of her to write about how I differ from my less talented brothers and sisters: my sister, Marceline, the witch; my lovely sister, Ura (pet name for Ursula) and my younger sister, Sanny, who played like an angel's harp on the boy's team at school.*

It would seem to be certain then that it was the character of Ursula he'd used to be Nick's sister in *The Last Good Country*. Ernest stayed in close contact with her throughout his life – even, later, when she moved to Honolulu. Ursula remained enthralled by her elder brother throughout her life – he was likewise in thrall of her, but this might have had to do with her being fascinated by him. This is underscored in the short story, in the words where she suggests they get married when they grow up.

There is further proof of her love for her brother in her almost submissive behavior shortly after her brother returns wounded from the war. Ursula was seventeen years old at the time and would sleep on the step outside Ernest's room door in order to be awake when he returned home. And when Ernest came Ursula wouldn't part from him even a slightest because she felt it was not good for a man to drink alone. She drank soft drinks with him until he fell asleep and then she slept by him to ensure he'd not be alone at night. They would sleep with the light on unless she switched it off after he'd gone to sleep, but she'd remain awake and switch the light on again if he woke up.

Hemingway himself wrote about it extensively and in detail. Between the lines there is evidence that Hemingway's war wounds were mental as well as physical, and perhaps Ursula was the only family member that he'd confided in on the extent of his injuries. This would explain her belief in the need to care for him on those long nights. Consequently, she was the one family member he'd loved most of all. Ursula's caring for the wellbeing of her brother, returning wounded from war, is remarkable. How appropriate it was shows a poem Hemingway wrote, in 1921, with the meaningful title: "*Killed Piave-July 8-1918*", the very day Hemingway was seriously wounded.

> Desire and
> All the sweet pulsing aches
> And gentle hurtings
> That were you,
> Are gone into the sullen dark.
>
> Now in the night you come unsmiling
> To lie with me
> A dull, cold, rigid bayonet
> On my hot-swollen, throbbing soul.
>
> Cover my eyes with your pinions
> Dark bird of night...
> Dip with your beak to my lips
> But cover my eyes with your pinions.

It is worth mentioning that after his death, Ursula set up the "Ernest Hemingway Memorial Award for the Creative Writing" at the University of Hawaii. She took her own life five years later when she found out that she had incurable cancer.

The Hemingway family established an unspeakably tragic "tradition" in which four of the eight family members, and one of Hemingway's granddaughters, committed suicide. At the age of forty-two, Margaux Hemingway took her life on the anniversary of her grandfather in 1996. Male members of the family: the father, Dr. Clarence Hemingway and sons, Ernest and Leicester took their lives in the same manner: they shot themselves.

The suicides of Ernest and Ursula become all the more tragic when one considers the brother, sister relationship, Nick and Littless – as they are called in the story. Despite ups and downs, they seem to wander through the natural world in a relatively carefree manner. There seems to be a future for them, albeit uncertain and seemingly impossible at times, but nonetheless part of their scheme of dreams – dreams that yearn for a bright and carefree future. These are two children living in harmony with nature; who see life as valuable and worth living. There are two scenes in the story, *The Last Good Country*, that throw light on their mutual attraction and on Ursula's sensitive nature. In the first, we become aware of the nostalgic sadness that escape from Horton Bay causes the brother and sister:

*When they were at the top of the hill they looked back and saw the lake in the moonlight. It was clear enough so they could see the dark point, and beyond there were the hills of the far shore.*
*"We might as well say goodbye to it," Nick Adams said.*
*"Goodbye, Lake," Littless said. "I love you, too."*

The second scene has to do with hunting. It shows that the passion for hunting is not just a question of upbringing and environment – it has more to do with character traits: Littless enjoyed the same upbringing and grew up in the same place, yet has reservations about hunting. This could, of course, also have to do with her being of a feminine nature:

*They had gone on and suddenly Nick had raised the rifle and shot before his sister could see what he was looking at. Then they heard the sound of a big bird tossing and beating it wings to the ground. She saw Nick pumping the gun and shoot twice more...*

*Nick went forward into the willows and picked up the three grouse and batted their heads against the butt of the rifle stock and laid them out on the moss. His sister felt them, warm and full-breasted and beautiful feathered.*

*"Wait till we eat them," Nick said. He was very happy.*

*"I'm sorry for them now," his sister said. "They were enjoying the morning just like we were."*

The sister seems to be lovable, but how about the character Nick, and what about Hemingway as a person? As author he is an exceptional personality – a writer of world renown whose work has survived way beyond his death and which will continue to shine. However, the person, Hemingway, could not be considered extraordinary – more the opposite. He behaved like one not committed to any values and that does not include his martial behavior that is reflected in the story *The Last Good Country*.

His was the life of a drunk. When one reads about Hemingway's childhood and youth one can sense tragedy approaching. The sensitivities displayed by the young author are clearly expressed in the passage when his character Littless, upon leaving, says to the lake: *I love you*, or the joy she felt in sharing outdoors in summer with her brother, or her feelings for all creatures – even the dead birds.

When one gets to know this landscape, the environment and Hemingway's love of it, it becomes clear that it was his refuge, especially in adolescence when it gave him the impulses needed for his life as an author. And when the unhappy circumstances of his immediate family are taken into account, it becomes easier to sympathize with his irresponsible behavior and restless nature that were part and parcel of his later life. With all this in mind, it is no longer possible to reproach him for having messed up his life – on the contrary, one must conclude that all these factors that led to his depressive disposition, were grounded in things outside of his literary success.

Even in his first few stories and in few words Hemingway was able to portray finely-drawn, life-like characters that many of his fellow authors were not able to. Another aspect that distinguishes him as a writer was his strong bond with the natural world. A writer like this, must be able to draw up from and have access to the depths of the soul – access to which remained shut to him in everyday life, where he blocked every action and experience. This sensitive aspect was missing in Hemingway's life, or rather he denied himself for fear he might not be seen to be the powerful man he would like to have considered himself to be. And when one considers a childhood of trying to compensate for a "weak father" and outdo a "domineering mother", how could he possibly have known anything else?

Ernest's relationship with his mother was described by Major General Charles T. Lanham who had been with him in the fronts of the Second World War:

*He always referred to his mother as "that bitch." He must have told me a thousand times how much he hated her and in how many ways.*[16]

From Hemingway's portrayal the real reasons are not all that clear. It seems certain that one of the reasons would have been the way she had treated his father. In his late thirties, Ernest wrote that he [the father] *was married to a woman with whom he had no more in common than a coyote has with a female poodle...*

Later, Ernest made her responsible for his father's suicide, but the actual reason for it could have had to do with the state of his father's health. He suffered from diabetes among other things. There were money problems as well. An unfortunate investment in Florida led to financial difficulties. According to the story told by Ernest's brother, Leicester, their father once had asked Ernest for money which he had sent immediately. The letter containing the money was delivered on the sixth of December in 1928 – the day Dr. Hemingway shot himself. His son's letter with the money lay unopened in his room.

Even if Ernest never did not go into detail on reasons why he had disliked his mother, we can draw our own conclusions when we look at the way she had behaved towards him. This behavior must have left scars on the son's soul.

She'd wanted him to be more feminine, more a twin sister for his sister Marceline who was a year his senior. The mother used to dress him in girl's clothes and treated him as a girl. From when they began to walk, boys and girls could be distinguished by clothing and hairstyles – but not Ernest. His mother, Grace, was determined to treat Ernest and his sister Marceline as twins and this only came to an end when Ernest began to attend kindergarten. But not only did Ernest and his sister wore the same clothes, they slept in identical beds in the same room. They had the same toy dolls and were encouraged by their mother to do everything together. Later she would send them for fishing trips, on walking tours or even visiting friends together. She wanted them not only to look like twins but to act like twins. She did everything in her power to ensure Ernest and Marceline could be together. She had them go out together as a twosome or made them a present of a season ticket for the opera. Even after Ernest had begun to go out with girls, she saw to it that they went to a student ball as a couple.

Her delusion reached a notable high point when she kept Marceline back a year in order that they could start school together. Ernest, however, did not feel drawn to his sister. And when, at the age of twenty-two, he's wanted to marry, his mother, concerned about the chill between him and his sister, and requested that he writes about it to Marceline. And furthermore, she worryingly suggested, Marceline was shattered, distraught and a bundle of nerves since she'd got to hear of the forthcoming wedding. But Ernest had no intention of writing. He was not particularly interested in sister's troubled soul and his feelings for her were anything but loving or brotherly. In a letter to his other sister, Sanny, in August 1949, he wrote:

*Marce I always thought, from when I first knew her, which goes back now half a hundred years, of as a bitch complete with handles, want nothing to do with her ever.*

In truth, Marceline must have felt herself to be in a situation not to her liking, because she did not attend Ernest's wedding – something that would not have, especially, disturbed the groom.

Anyone who'd taken an interest in the family or who had known them in any way could not have been in doubt about the manipulative influence the mother had on her son. In biographies, one can read that he willingly played the role of "sister" to his sister, albeit insisting on his sexuality. But, as the choice of clothes in their holiday times in Michigan shows, the mother was also not always consistent in her wish to have Ernest behave as a girl.

From early childhood having an identical sister was a deep-seated disturbance in Hemingway's definition of his own self. His sexual identity and physical awareness culminated in the question: "am I a boy or a girl?" or "what am I, or what am I not?" When a boy is confused about his *ego*, his body and his sexual identity, it has far-reaching consequences for his later development and, in particular, for his relationship with the opposite sex.

It would appear as if the ill-feeling between Ernest and his mother reached its highest point after his return from the war in Europe. On his return there was constant criticism of his rejection of her wish that he should have gone to college. To make matters worse, his mother was in bad physical condition. She was plagued with headaches and gout in her shoulders and arms. It was in this atmosphere that Ernest spent his time at home trying to write short stories, all of which were rejected by publishers. When he wasn't writing he was amusing himself with friends.

In early summer 1919, the Hemingway family went, as always, to Michigan. The tension between mother and son was growing. In her eyes he was behaving like a stubborn child that didn't help out at home and who did nothing but sit in the corner smoking and reading, or buzzing about the place with his friend Bill in his car, or going out with a red-haired high-school girl by the name of Marjorie. As against that, Ernest felt really annoyed and upset by the fact that despite all the experiences he'd had in his life, his mother still treated him as a little boy.

And in other respects his mother was strange, especially when it came to the essence of motherly love. One can get a grasp of her state of mind from a letter she gave her twenty-one year old son a year later, when she threw him out of the house in Windemere, after an argument.

She must have spent considerable time thinking about what she'd say to him – one can assume it was carefully thought out. She strangely compares in that letter a mother's love to a bank account – a support fund that is drawn upon for the first five years. During this time, so to speak, the mother is a kind of biological slave. Afterwards the account continues to be drawn upon, albeit in smaller quantities. It is expected that some deposits are to be made: such as a willingness to do favors or to be considerate or to say "thank you" now and then. After puberty the account is noticeably empty, but it continues to pay out in the form of love and understanding. But now, according to Ernest's mother, the time has come to begin "to pay back" – and this in large sums. There is a general payback list which, sometimes, becomes detailed and demanding. Examples would be: take home flowers, fruit, snacks, something pretty to wear or greet the mother with a kiss or an embrace. Perhaps bills could be, quietly, paid to take some of the pressure off the mother. Grace knows of mothers who get all of these and more from their sons – from her own son though she gets none of these things. The account overdraft comparison is followed by reproaches. She refers to his ancestry: "you come from a line of gentlemen." And at the end she expresses the hope that he will come to his senses and should this happen, salvation in the form of love could await him. It's hard to believe but the letter does exist. One can only conclude that she is a sad woman who had been deeply disappointed in her life.

As a young girl, Grace had been a very talented singer who, with the full support of her parents, was able to concentrate on her music lessons. It was felt she had enough talent to have a career as an opera singer. She was being prepared for a life on stage. When she had graduated from High School she taught music and, at the same time, kept up her voice training. However, her hopes of a great career did not materialize. In spring of 1896 she had her debut in Madison Square Garden, New York, where she suffered such severe headaches that she gave up rather than not succeed. Against the better judgment of her singing teacher, she ended her career and married Dr. Clarence Hemingway. Having been brought up to stay out of the kitchen as much as she could, she was, all at once, living the life of a housewife.

The dreams of a great career were over and these expectations unfulfilled and frustrated. A woman who has reached such a heightened pitch or position in life will often try to live out their own failed ambitions in their children. The husband, not understanding or knowing these unfulfilled needs, is often more in the way than anything else.

Instead of providing the children with love and care, they become objects of special study. The necessary care and attention is governed by how they are expected to behave. In general, Hemingway's relationship with his mother could be considered problematic to very bad. It doesn't change in his adult life – even to her death. He even stayed away from his mother's funeral.

The situation was different with his father. Ernest rejected him as well, because he saw him as a coward. But the weakness in his father that he rejected, he attributed to his mother. If there is not a deep emotional bond with the mother, it can be difficult for the child with and for the father. A more intense reading of the story, *Fathers and Sons*, reveals to us how much Ernest must have loved his father. The story was published in 1933, five years after his father's death, in the short story collection, *Winner Take Nothing*.

The story deals with grandfather, father and son, and the relationship between the grandfather and his son and that of the father and his own boy. Nick Adams drives about the countryside with his young son. He remembers his own father who'd introduced him to fishing and hunting; he recalls his father's helplessness in explaining the facts of life to him, most importantly he remembers him as a great hunter.

When Hemingway created the character of Nick's father, one can assume that the events and happenings in his young life can be superimposed on the life of the young Hemingway. In the story though he writes with affection about his father:

*He was sentimental, and, like most sentimental people, he was both cruel and abused... All sentimental people are betrayed so many times... Nick was a boy and he was very grateful to him fort two things, fishing an shooting. His father was a sound on those two things as he was unsound of sex, for instance, and Nick was glad that it has been that way; for someone has to give you your first gun or the opportunity to get it and use it, and you have to live where there is game or fish if you are to learn about them, and now, at thirty-eight, he loved to fish and to shoot exactly as much as when he first have gone with his father.*

Despite being deprived and his emotional needs not being met by his father's strictness, it is understandable that the young man, until he was sixteen, grew up only with sisters, desperately held on to his love of his father. There were opportunities for his father to have been there for him; opportunities to pass on his knowledge and experiences to his son as something special. In these special moments, there is the manly side of his father; the part that was usually hidden behind a domineering wife; moments when the father fulfilled deep longings in his son. On the death of Hemingway's father, F. Scott Fitzgerald wrote to him and Ernest replied in a letter from December, ninth in 1928: *I was fond as hell of my father and feel too punk – also sick etc. – to write a letter but wanted to thank you.*

The father, when he could show his fatherly feelings, was loved by Ernest, liked and honored. But the mother was always in-between the two of them. It was a terrible setup where a son felt drawn to a father who, in turn, was put down and humiliated by a mother, who saw her son as "an investment." Did Ernest really have a chance of a better childhood – a chance to not to become a victim of dependency and of depression in his later life?

How could a growing boy or youth come to terms with all of this? On the one hand he has a father who means everything to him, but a father who is subservient to his wife, on the other. The youth called this as a "betrayal" and considered his father therefore a "coward." His father's suicide in 1928 supports this insight: because to end ones own life means not to accept it and to withdraw from it. Ernest's father shot himself as in his elderly life did Ernest, who in doing so failed in his lifelong wish *not to be* like his father.

So, Hemingway's path towards Nobel Prize had its own price; the price for his fame and his extraordinary talent as a writer. He himself saw this Prize as the result and outcome of an unhappy childhood and youth. And when one adds that the conditions of that time were male domination, and the first experience of adult man's life was war, it is understandable that the masculine side of Ernest's personality was over-emphasized. Hemingway was severely injured in The First World War and honored for his bravery. These experiences preoccupied him throughout his life and their impact is to be seen in his work.

He lived the life of a public hero perhaps placing too much emphasis on the body at the expense of his soul. Even from early youth, alcohol had been the substance that had masked the division of body and soul in him but, as in most cases, it only appears to "help" in the short term.

The suffering that followed resulted in depression. If the illness does not find its way out, the life of a man becomes a torment and suicide offers an immediate "solution" to the suffering or an "escape".

In order not to appear a failure he had to *punch above his weight* in all areas and aspects of life. This involved a lot of pretense, playacting and talking himself up – and these character traits he possessed in abundance. All other qualities of his was left to its own devices. Outpouring masculinity was the attribute he played out in public and to the world. This was his "controlled" life and one which he seemed to believe he had fully mastered.

But the world was not as Hemingway imagined it to be and his behavior was not only admired. Continuing to paint a picture of himself and others was a laborious and exacting task and the effect he'd wanted to achieve was not always possible. In some respects people around him were compassionate and sympathetic to him in his role of victim, but it is an illusion that one can lead a life of always expecting to please others or of trying to prove something to himself.

Hemingway's preparation for the ending of his life on the morning of that summer's day in Ketchum, Idaho, was a confirmation of the worst possible fears for those closest to him. His wife, Mary, slept as he went out on to the verandah – his hunting shotgun loaded with two cartridges in his hands. He pulled both triggers at once. A short time previously, Mary had found him motionless with a gun in his hand and had taken it from him. He had tried to jump from a plane on one occasion and on another, he had almost deliberately run into a rotating propeller just as the plane was about to take off. One day though… he hit the "target".

For the world as large Hemingway probably showed only his manly side focused on brevity. The reason perhaps was that his insecurity about his sexual identity, caused by mother's attempt to bring him up as his sister Marceline's twin, would have influenced his understanding of manhood. This would, furthermore, have been compounded by a "weak" father who had been unable to be a manly example. Ernest had four sisters. His brother, Leicester, was sixteen years his junior which meant that apart from his father he was surrounded by female members of the family. Hemingway didn't want to be seen as weak or feminine. He had to appear to be manly because from earliest childhood he had to suppress what he'd hated most in his father – cowardice.

But not only Hemingway's suicide shows that it had been difficult for him to avoid the inevitable. After his death, Norman Mailer attested to it in an essay written for the magazine *The Esquire* and entitled, "The Big Bite:"

*Probably Hemingway was not the brave man, who was searching the smell of trouble for the sake of the feelings that would be conveyed. The truth about his odyssey is probably just that he has fought all his life against cowardice and a hidden secret to commit suicide, and that his inner landscape was a nightmare. He might spent his nights in wrestling with the deities. It could even be, that the final evaluation of his work, came to the conclusion, that his failure was tragical, but his work heroic. It can not be ruled out, that he carried fears around that would have suffocated any weaker man than him.*[17]

This opinion, in words of a professional, sums up the twilight years of the gifted writer, Hemingway. His tragic end would suggest that he found the discrepancy between the public life he led and his true inner person, intolerable. If his work reflects on something wholly, it is the meaninglessness of many aspects of life and the ruthlessness of death.

He had offered his services as an ambulance man behind the front line in First World War. Later, in the Spanish Civil war he took a bank loan to afford the opportunity of supporting his literary voice and activity for the cause of the freedom fighters. He was a war correspondent in the Second World War. He went on countless big game hunting expeditions in Africa and survived two plane crashes.

It might be, as he himself said, that an unhappy childhood is the very best preparation for the life of a good writer, but, by the same token, his later life might, also, have helped him to become the great writer.

All this taken into account, it is not difficult to understand and consider the nature and style of Hemingway's life, to be a sacrifice for literature.

Ernest Hemingway's formation and upbringing did not make him into the brave and sturdy youth he saw himself to be, but rather someone who was much more sensitive and anxious, as can be deduced from the story, *Three Shots*:

*He was always a little frightened of the woods at night. He opened the flap of the tent and undressed an lay very quietly between the blankets in the dark. The fire was burnt down to a bed of coals outside. Nick lay still and tried to go to sleep. There was no noise anywhere. Nick felt he could only hear the fox bark or an owl or anything he would be all right. He was not afraid of anything definite as yet. But he was getting very afraid...*

*Last night in the tent he had had the same fear. He never had it except at night. It was more a realization than a fear at first. But it was always on the edge of fear and became fear very quickly when it started. As soon as he began to be really frightened he took the rifle and poked the muzzle out the front of the tent and shot three times...*

*He lay down to wait for his father's return and was asleep before his father and uncle put out their jack light on the other side of the lake.*

The literature on Hemingway is full of shades of psychological assumptions and conclusions, such as castration fears or fetishes, which are gone into in great detail in the book, *Hemingway's Fet-*

*ishism: Psychoanalysis and the Mirror of Manhood.* His preference for youthful-looking women with short haircuts is referred to;
also racial fetishism that is claimed it can be read between the
lines of the manuscript, *The Garden of Eden*, which was published
after Hemingway's death. This is also referred to in Nick Adam's
stories, where Nick has his first sexual encounter with the Indian
maiden, Prudence Boulton.

Hemingway had grown up with sisters and was, therefore, no
stranger to the physical difference between boys and girls – especially with all their freedom and running about in summer months,
these differences could not have remained unnoticed. Ernest's father had taught him not only fishing and hunting, but also swimming – at the same time as Marceline. This would have satisfied
the mother's "twin-wish" although the father appeared to have
been against the idea.

It was a special privilege for the Hemingway children in summer
in Michigan, to go swimming, naked, just before bedtime; a habit
they kept up into teenage years. Apart from the unverified incestuous relationship Ernest should had had with his sister Ursula, it
would appear that the first girl he'd seen, in puberty, had been
Prudence Boulton, that Indian girl. She was the daughter of Nick
Boulton who, like all the Indians, worked at the sawmill. Boulton
is introduced in the first sentence of the story, *The Doctor and the
Doctor's Wife* – where, however, he is referred to as Dick:

*Dick Boulton came from the Indian camp to cut up logs for Nick's
father. He brought hiss on Eddy and another Indian Bill Tabeshaw
with him.*

The story is interesting because, in the course of the story, the Indian accuses Nick's father of stealing timber, although he had explained that it had simply been a floating log that had fallen off a
transport ship. He thought it better to take it out of the water than
to let it rot. The Indian insisted that Nick's father had stolen the
timber, which resulted in a quarrel and the Indians being sent
away. It is possible that the incident did take place because the ar-

gument that ensued between Nick's parents would indicate that Nick's mother (like Ernest's) was a practicing Christian who advised her husband to stay out of fights and arguments.

This story, published in 1924, in the journal *Transatlantic*, was praised by Ernest's father for the very first time that he did about a text written by his son. This is indeed confusing because, in the journal, Dr. Hemingway is not portrayed in a positive light. Neither in the fight with the Indians where he is portrayed as a loud-mouth, nor in conversation with his wife where he meekly capitulates.

Apparently Ernest's father considered the story to be purely fictitious, because, in real life, the Indian would have chopped up the old tree trunk and the fight would not have taken place.

In a letter to his son, Dr. Hemingway praised him for his story and the fact that, as far as he could remember, Ernest would have been as young as twelve years old at the time of the incident. And in the letter, he also writes he'd be delighted if Ernest could send him some of his work more often. In the light of all that had happened earlier, this wish was incomprehensible. Shortly before this, Dr. Hemingway had sent his son's book titled *in our time* back to the publisher.

The book in question was that little thirty-two page book printed in Paris in 1924. In 1925, the following year, it was published in America with the same title. But this time, the style of the title had changed into capital letters, *In Our Time*. Ernest parents ordered six copies from the first book. After reading it, especially the lines where the character in the book, a war hero like Ernest, had infected gonorrhea from a salesgirl, they sent all of them back, because, as Dr. Hemingway wrote, they didn't wish to keep such "filth" in the house.

Ernest was delighted by his father's praise of his story, *The Doctor and the Doctor's Wife*, and he wrote to him from Paris on March the twentieth, 1925:

*I am so glad you liked the Doctor story. I put in Dick Boulton and*

*Billy Tabeshaw as real people with their real names because it was pretty sure they would never read the Transatlantic Review. I've written a number of stories about the Michigan country – the country is always true – what happens in the stories is fiction.*

As later letters show, this recognition by his father, which had delighted Hemingway at the beginning of his career, was an exception. On February the fifth, 1927, in a letter to his mother, but addressed to both father and mother, he states that he finds it pitiful that he as an author has to justify himself to his parents. He wants to write books and not letters to his parents. If his books are not to their liking, perhaps that can change one day, because:

*You may never like any thing I write and than suddenly, you might like something very much.*

Ernest was not ashamed of his work. Why should he have been? But he felt obliged to emphasize this in a letter to his mother: *otherwise, I am in no way ashamed at all of the book.*

His mother couldn't or wouldn't accept what her son was doing. The public recognition his work was receiving changed nothing for her. That letter was referring to the book, *The Sun Also Rises*, which was a huge success. This shame that he didn't feel, was justified by the quality of his writing. He would only be ashamed if he didn't do his work properly; if he didn't quite capture the people and their character he'd been trying to describe or if they didn't come alive in the eye of the reader. And even if – he says it himself – the book is unpleasant or uncomfortable, it is not all that unpleasant; it is not more unpleasant than the real lives of some of the leading families in Oak Park, Chicago where the Hemingway family lived.

Hemingway had to point out to his mother things that he as a writer took for granted and which were understood by the neutral reader of sound mind: books dealt with the dark underbelly of life and questioned what is acceptable, because in public day-to-day life, people attempt to show themselves up only in their best light. He tried to get his mother to see his point of view when he addressed the artist in her. She should try to realize that an author must not be forced to defend his outlook on the world, but, on the other hand, he must be open to criticism of his writing.

Nobody can avoid having the impression that Ernest couldn't grasp why his mother still moaned, criticized and grumbled about him even though he was a recognized author. It must have been intolerable for him not being able to convince this unsympathetic woman of his wonderful talent as a writer. It must have been similar to an author having to appear before a censorship tribunal.

For Ernest, his father was different. Compared to his mother, he had, at least, behaved loyally, although Ernest had felt his father had not liked his books, as a letter dated on September the fourteenth, 1927 suggested:

*I know you don't like the sort of thing I write but this is the difference in our taste...*

He was right of course, and this includes not only different people but also differing attitudes towards every single person as, for instance, can be seen in Hemingway's taste in women.

This has been carefully researched by biographers – many of whom describe his preference for dark-skinned women. Their descriptions are preoccupied with that Indian girl, Prudy (Prudence) Boulton, who had worked from time to time as a housekeeper at the Hemingway summer home. She was three years younger than Ernest and in her free time she went hunting for squirrels with her brother Billy and Ernest.

The story *Fathers and Sons* shows how Prudy is connected to the character of Nick. In the story she is Trudy:

*But there were still much forest then, virgin forest where the trees grow high before there were any branches and you walked on the brown, clean springy-needled ground with no underground and it was cool on the hottest days and they three lay against a trunk of a hemlock wider then two beds are long, with the breeze high in the tops and the cool light that came in patches, and Billy said:*
*"You want Trudy again?"*

*"You want to?"*
*"Un huh."*
*"Come on."*
*"No, here."*
*"But Billy –"*
*"I no mind Billy. He my brother."*
*Than afterwards they sat, the three of them, listening for a black squirrel that was in the top branches where they could not see him.*

That Hemingway allowed his Nick Adams to have sex with Trudy becomes more obvious in other scenes:

*Than later, it was along time after and Billy was still away.*
*"You think we make a baby?" Trudy folded her brown legs together happily and rubbed against him. Something inside Nick had gone a long way away.*
*"I don't think so," he said.*
*"Make plenty baby what the hell."*

The biographer Constance Cappel tells in her book's preface *Sweetgrass and Smoke*, she has been struck by Prudence Boulton's tragic life. The young girl died in February 1918 in a double suicide pact with an ex-convict named Richard or Jim Castle. She may have been pregnant at the time of her death. Boulton is buried in an unmarked grave in the Greensky Church cemetery on Susan Lake in northern Michigan.

In 1950, Hemingway raved about a dark-skinned beauty he'd spent an evening with. She'd worn a fur coat and nothing but a fur coat. This woman was Josephine Baker, an American-born French dancer, singer, and actress that was the first African-American woman to star in a major motion picture, Zouzou (1934). The story is, most probably, not true but would seem to suggest his preference for dark-skinned women. As others, noble prize awarded writer Toni Morrison – herself dark-skinned – would have noticed this in his posthumously published novel manuscript, *The Garden of Eden*. That's why the fantasy of sexual initiation with the Indian maiden, Trudy (Prudy) presents us with greater complexity than simply nostalgia. He, the white youth, grants himself the right to consider an Indian girl as a sexual object, but, conversely, threatens an Indian youth with murder when he makes advances to a white girl – which can be seen in another passage where Trudy's brother Billy tells of his half-brother's wishes:

*"Eddie says he going to come some night sleep in bed with your sister Dorothy."*

*"What?"*

*"He said."*

*Trudy nodded.*

*"That's all he want do," she said. Eddie was their older half brother. He was seventeen.*

*"If Eddie Gilby ever comes at night and even speaks to Dorothy you know what I'm do to him? I'd kill him like this." Nick cocked the gun and hardly taking aim pulled the trigger, blowing a hole as big as your hand in the head of the belly of that half-breed bastard Eddie Gilby.*

*"Like that. I'd kill him like that."*

*"He better not come then," Trudy said. She put her hand in Nick's pocket.*

*"He better watch out plenty," said Billy.*

*"He is big bluff," Trudy was exploring with her hand in Nick's pocket.*

*"But don't you kill him. You got plenty trouble."*

In his Hemingway biography, Kenneth S. Lynn believes: *Prudy may have fallen in habit in putting an exploring hand in Ernest's pocket while the three of them sat quietly in the middle of the woods listening for squirrels in the top branches; she may even have lain on her back on a bed of pine needles and allowed Ernest to climb on top of her while Billy watched.*

He says it would appear to be the truth, but if he doesn't have sources, other than this book, there is nothing to go on. We know that Prudy did exist and we, also, know that she and her brother spent time with Ernest. Apart from that, we have nothing to go on. Lynn, however, goes on to say:

*The truth may lie somewhere in between. It would appear that, for a time at least, before Prudy started having more serious liaisons with older white boys and mature men like the fellow from Charlevoix with whom she would eventually make a death pact, Ernest thought of her as his girl and that their encounters in the woods were not entirely platonic.*

The biographer, Carlos Baker added:

*Ernest's fictional accounts of sexual initiation with Prudy Boulton were more likely the product of wishful thinking than of fact.*

But even if the stories of Hemingway's sexual awakening and experiences with the Indian girl are not true, it would appear as if he felt very attracted to her. In *Ten Indians*, Nick thinks of an Indian girl, called Prudy Mitchell. Here again, there is explicit evidence of racial prejudice and of the low esteem in which Indians were held by white Americans. This is very clear from the conversation on the coach when Joe Garner has to shove drunken Indians, who are blocking the road, to one side and also from this part:

*Nick sat between the two boys. The road came out into a clearing.*
*"Right here was where Pa ran over the skunk."*
*"It was further on."*
*"It don't make no difference where it was," Joe said without turning his head. "One place is just as good as another to run over a skunk."*
*"I saw two skunks last night," Nick said.*
*"Where?"*
*"Down by the lake. They were looking for dead fish along the beach."*
*"They were coons probably," Carl said.*
*"They were skunks. I guess I know skunks."*
*"You ought to," Carl said. "You got an Indian girl."*
*"Stop talking that way, Carl," said Mrs. Garner.*
*"Well, they smell about the same."*

*Joe Garner laughed.*

*"You stop laughing, Joe," Mrs. Garner said. "I won't have Carl talk that way."*

*"Have you got an Indian girl, Nickie," Joe asked.*

*"No."*

*"He has too, Pa," Frank said. "Prudence Mitchell's his girl."*

*"She's not."*

*"He goes to see her every day."*

*"I don't."* Nick, sitting between the two boys in the dark, felt hollow and happy inside himself to be teased about Prudence Mitchell.

When Nick finally gets home, his father tells him he has seen Prudence with a youth in the woods and they were really amusing themselves. Nick enquires further:

*"What were they doing?"*

*"I didn't stay to find out."*

*"Tell me what they were doing."*

*"I don't know," his father said. "I just heard them threshing around."*

*"Who was it with her?" Nick asked.*

*"Frank Washburn."*

*"Were they – were they –"*

*"Were they what?"*

*"Were they happy?"*

*"I guess so."...*

*Nick went into his room, undressed, and got into bed. He heard his father moving around in the living room. Nick lay in his bed with his face in the pillow.*

*'My heart is broken,' he thought. 'If I feel this way my heart must be broken.'*

Prudy Boulton is the first female with whom Ernest Hemingway is associated. There are readers who are convinced that Ernest had his first sexual experience with her. Others are equally convinced that Hemingway's account of his sexual initiation with her is fiction through and through and that this so-called encounter was nothing more to it than a good friendship.

But like many readers, Hemingway's widow, has always regarded Nick's testimony as a reflection of real-life fact. Prudy Boulton was the first girl my husband ever "pleasured," as she asserts in her autobiography. (She also did not doubt him when he told her in a London restaurant in 1944 that her legs were just like Prudy's.)[18]

From the accounts of his sexual encounters with an Indian girl, it is deduced that Hemingway preferred dark-skinned woman – a theory supported by the manuscript, *The Garden of Eden*. From this and other publications and statements, a whole assortment of fetishes, oedipal castration anxieties, preference for androgynous beings or homophobic tendencies are attributed to him. It may be that Hemingway's upbringing, especially his mother's twins-phobia of bonding him with his sister, led to a disposition to fetishism of a kind. In his youth and as a young adult, his preference for black women or otherwise is not supported by concrete evidence as such – with the exception of his preference for older women, but which was later repudiated and even the reverse shown to be true.

As in consideration of the role of women in Hemingway's work, distinctions can be made as, indeed, it comes to his four wives. The subjugation of the barmaid, Liz, in the story *Up in Michigan*, is an aspect of this. He describes her as naïve and overcome by infatuation. In the story he outlines his perception of manhood when he makes it clear to Liz that men and women consider sex and love in much different ways.

We find Nick Adams who's character reminds Hemingway in his adulthood; a man who has great difficulty in having a long and fruitful relationship with a woman who will not, or cannot be subservient to him. Three of his wives fitted this pattern. It began with Hadley who had supported him at the beginning and who had tolerated her husband flirting with other women in her presence –

even to the point where he'd practically moved in with Pauline Pfeiffer. She would become his second wife when Hadley could no longer stand it.

The last wife, Mary Walsh, who became his widow, lived up to the image of the faithful wife, although she must have known of Hemingway's reputation and his treatment of women, which could not have been any different at the time of their marriage.

The only wife that broke the mold was Martha Gellhorn. According to Hemingway, this marriage broke up because she concentrated too much of her energy on her career as a war correspondent. In 1954, many years after they'd been divorced, he asked himself how she managed now that there's no war.

During the war in 1943, while still married to her, Hemingway was not at all happy when his wife left him alone to travel to Europe to work in her profession as correspondent. By the standards of the present, it would be normal for a woman to travel to a war zone to work as reporter, but in those days, not only was Hemingway annoyed – the American Government was not at all happy either to have a female war correspondent.

After the war, Gellhorn was one of the first journalists to report on the Concentration Camp in Dachau. She has been described as one of the *great* war correspondents and since 1999 the "Martha Gellhorn Prize for Journalism" is awarded. In April 2008, she was honored by the *American Post* when she was one of five journalists to be included in the special 41-cent stamp.

She had been too independent for Hemingway and he got revenge in his own way. In 1943/44 against Hemingway's wish she travelled, alone, to Europe and although she had expressly asked him to accompany her, he had refused but, instead, bombarded her with letters full of tears and longing.

When she finally did accede to his wish to return to their *Finca* home in Cuba, she found him in a terrible state surrounded by a host of combat drinkers. He had grown a bushy beard and was in a nasty and confrontational state. There was no suggestion of his being happy to see her again. Neither was there a trace of gratitude that she had returned earlier than expected, although he knew her greatest wish had been to have remained in Europe for the expected invasion on D-Day, allied forces invasion day to the occupied France.

She could have spared herself this return. There was nothing but fights and, even worse, Hemingway humiliated her. While she'd been in Europe, where he'd not wanted to go or accompany her, he'd – overstepping her – signed a contract with *Colliers Weekly* – a magazine for which Martha had written and published two hundred and thirty articles between 1938 and 1943. Now he was the one flying first class to Europe, while she chugged along in the bunk of a Norwegian freight ship transport divers and dynamite to Europe.

That's how he was and that's how he grew as a future man. The characters of women and girls we meet in the *Nick Adams Stories* are drawn from real people: Ernest's sister Ursula, Kate Smith, Marjorie Bump and Prudy Boulton. These girls knew a different Ernest. In the story, *Ten Indians*, Prudy Boulton broke Nick's tender heart. In this, otherwise, so unspoiled Michigan, he seemed so completely innocent. But guilt, as the opposite, lay in waiting and it made out of him – what would have seemed impossible from this writing – the macho Hemingway who had behaved in such a despicable manner to his wife Martha Gellhorn. He was one of the boys, the man of man's to the marrow.

But the soul of a sincere young man shone through the young Ernest, in the image of Nick, who had experienced depression and melancholy in his youth and who had entered adult life weighed down with these experiences. The loss of "life in Paradise" is accompanied with melancholy for almost anyone, and it would not have been any different for Ernest. His Paradise lasted just a few summers. He was driven out of it and when he achieved fame, he couldn't ever find it again. Later, "East of Eden," he was frightened of living.

In January 1919, having returned from The First World War in Europe, Hemingway moved to his parent's home in Oak Park. In a made-to-measure uniform, but needing a walking stick, he was met by his father and sister, Marceline, at the station in Chicago. He was hoping for a marriage with Agnes von Kurowsky, a nurse he had met while in the army hospital in Milan. He had enjoyed the company of the Red Cross nurses at the hospital, but Agnes had been his favorite. She was a tall, dark-haired woman eight years his senior. All the men were taken by her, but it was Hemingway who had, apparently, won her favor. He was a war hero and the first American to be heroically injured in Italy. He fell deeply in love with her but, in a letter dated March 1919, she, bluntly, informed him that she was to marry another: *It has come as a surprise, believe me: I am soon to be married.*

But that would not have been the worst part of the letter. She began by saying she'd still had a lot of feelings for him (*I am still very fond of you*) but more the feelings *of a mother than a sweetheart.*

A disaster. His war wounds were hardly healed when Ernest's heart gets broken. He had really loved this woman. In March 1919 and on the very same day as he'd received the letter from Agnes, he wrote to his friend, Bill Horne expressing his very deep feelings for her.

A few extracts where he pours out his feelings: *She doesn't love me, Bill. She takes it all back. A "mistake." One of those little mistakes, you know. But Bill, I've loved Ag. She is been my ideal, and Bill, I forgot all about religion and everything else because I had Ag. to worship. All I wanted was Ag. And I'm writing this with a dry mouth and a lump in the old throat, and Bill I wish you were here to talk to. I hope he's (the man she is going to marry) the best man in the world. Aw, Bill, I can't write about it cause I do love her so damn much.*[19]

But, as is often the case in life, he got his second chance. The time had not been right or he had been too much injured, or perhaps a little of both. In 1919 he went to pick up his post from the General Store in Horton Bay and, to his surprise, there was a letter from Agnes. She wrote: *that her Duke's mother had refused to permit his marriage to an "American adventuress" and that Nicky (his name) had decided to do what his mother said. Throughout the letter, Agnes hinted that she had learned the difference between love and opportunity, and wouldn't it be fine if Ernest were her beau again.*[20]

Perhaps Hemingway had had a few sleepless nights but, as far as we know, he never replied. He outlined his reasons why in June sixteenth, 1919 in a letter to Howell C. Jenkins, who has driven ambulances with Ernest:

'*I loved her once and then she gypped me. And I don't blame her. But I set out cauterize out her memory and I burnt it out with a course of booze and other women and now it's gone.*'

As far as we can judge, only Marjorie was in his life at the time, and more than enough has already been written about their relationship.

After Agnes' "rejection," Hemingway set out for Michigan where he spent the years 1919/20 around Horton Bay and Petoskey when not with his family at Windemere. In these two years he fished extensively, also on the Upper Michigan Peninsula. He was preoccupied with reading and writing, and stayed on at Windemere when his family had left after the usual summer vacation in 1919. His mother threw him out of Windemere in summer 1920 and that was the time when he received the letter from Agnes. Afterwards, he was to return to Michigan just once, and that was to celebrate his wedding and honeymoon with Hadley Richardson in 1921.

Michigan was the one place where Ernest Hemingway could recover from the wounds of war and a broken relationship – the breakup with Agnes had been very painful. She had been his first great love and his first real disappointment. Afterwards, it would appear that Hemingway managed to avoid the pain of rejection by ensuring that he met someone new before ending the old relationship. At least, this appeared to be the case when it came to his wives. However, in 1919, first, in Horton Bay and, later, in Petoskey he comforted himself with Marjorie.

In Horton Bay he moved in with Liz Dilworth and her husband, Jim, who was the blacksmith. This is the very house where Ernest two years later was to celebrate his wedding with Hadley. In the winter of 1919 and 1920, he moved to the Potter's Rooming House – a guesthouse in 602 State Street, Petoskey – where he worked on his first short stories. His stay there is worth mentioning because it was this town that he located his first published novel, *The Torrents of Spring*, in 1925.

The contents of that book is strange: and bizarre. There is the character Scripps, who sets out on the lonely train tracks in the direction of Chicago in driving snow, but gets no further than Petoskey. There he enters "Browns Bean Bar" and consumes hot beans. A no longer young barmaid – Diana – is serving, and becomes later his wife. She then spends the day as Ms. Scripps at home. Lucky until she becomes aware of Mandy, the young bar-maid from the Beanery, who draws attention to herself with pretentious, stuck-up discussions with Scripps about fiction. Diana tries to get her husband back and subscribes to literary magazines to compete, but can't hold on to Scripps. He drops her and turns his attention to the more attractive Mandy.

Petoskey has got a pump factory, where Scrubs finds labor and where he met Yogi. When it began to snow, Yogi and the other workers leave Petoskey and the pump factory. Yogi meets two Indians on an open field and while he tells them about his experiences of war, they remain silent. But then one of the Indians says they are war veterans, and he had been a major. The weather improves and all three return to Petoskey. They then take Yogi to a secret Indian club, but when Yogi admits he is no Native American all of them are thrown out of the club.

A number of unusual characters have gathered in Browns Bean Bar. A naked Indian came in out of the cold late-winter night with her baby and was immediately thrown out into the snow from which she rises and goes away. Yogi takes off his clothes and goes after her naked. The two Indians follow, gather Yogi's clothes and head back to Petoskey carrying the bundle.

The whole affair is grotesque in form and content. It is Hemingway's most unusual book and as a matter of fact it is a parody on Sherwood Anderson's bestseller, *Dark Laughter,* published in 1925. What makes this book special is something else: it marks the beginning of a life-long collaboration between Hemingway and the publishing house, Charles Scribner's Sons. Hemingway had first offered the book to the American publishers, Boni and Liveright, but they had rejected it because they were publishing books by Sherwood Anderson. It is suggested that Hemingway had written the book simply to extradite himself from his obligations to Boni and Liveright. His first wife Hadley remembers:

*'Ernest had talked to Scott about Scribner's and wanted to go there. He had a commitment to Liveright and wanted to get out of*

*it, so he wrote The Torrents of Spring satirizing their top author, Anderson. I know that Ernest didn't really want to write the book in order to change publishers, but Pauline (his second wife) wanted him to do it, and so he did.'[21]*

Traces of Hemingway are to be found in Petoskey all over. It is possible to imagine him leaving Potters House on State Street to walk to the public library, or he'd walk to the station to check timetables for future trips and buy the Chicago Tribune. He could be in Brown's Beanery for lunch or he, as people still do today, could have stood looking into the river from the Bear River Bridge.

What impression did he make on people from this tiny place at the time? Was he simply a man who spent his days writing and drinking too much? And would his international fame have impressed these people when he became well-known; the same people who had experienced him as a young man without money, and seen him hanging around the barber's shop telling yarns and stories. He would have loaf about waiting for schoolgirls to walk them home; spent time with one, Grace Quinlan, or evenings in the kitchen eating popcorn with another, Marjorie Bump, or telling both of them his best stories. What would people, who had known him at that time and still remembered him, have thought? It is difficult to say, but possible to imagine that, when he did spend time in Petoskey, he would not have presented a picture of a man in possession of a special talent as a writer – probably more of one trying to find an identity for himself; of one uncertain of his task in life, who had already experienced too much to be innocent and likeable. If he did draw attention to himself, it would not have been because of his special talent. Later he would report that during his time in Petoskey, he had spent the whole of autumn and half of winter writing, without being able to sell a thing. It was his training ground and apprenticeship.

This was an era of discouraging rejections. His first publication, *Three Stories and Ten Poems* – a short novel, published in 1923 in a print run of 300 copies, was partially financed by himself. In the following year, 1924, his short story collection, *in our time*, was published in an even smaller print run of 174 copies. The path to *The Old Man and the Sea*, for which he won the Nobel Prize in 1960 or prior to this amazing achievement, *For Whom the Bells Tolls*, a novel about people in the Spanish Civil War, had not been smooth. The latter, published in 1940, was sold out in three days in a print run of 75,000 copies. *The New York Times* called it the "best, deepest and truest book" that Hemingway had written.[22]

We learn about the genesis of *For Whom the Bell Tolls* in letters from Martha Gellhorn. In 1940, she wrote to the American novelist and poet, Hortense Flexner:

*'I read the last parts of E's book last night. He is like an animal in his writing; he keeps it all in one drawer, close to him, and hides it under other papers, and never willingly shows it and cannot bear to talk about it. It is of course an absolute marvel, far and away the finest thing he has done and probably one of the great war books of always. It is so exact that it becomes truer than life, and yet it is all invented.'*[23]:

To suggest that it's all a figment of the imagination is not quite true. Hemingway, himself, said that a good writer can only write about what he has personally experienced. He had first-hand knowledge of war: he had been seriously injured in The First World War and had been a war correspondent in the Spanish Civil war. Martha refers to the plot. Here it is seen it is not enough to have had lots of experiences; the writer must have the imagination to create the story out of it and this is something that reaches back to early childhood. As we know, Hemingway had always been able "to spin yarns," to tell stories and not only those found in his books. The extent to which Martha had helped Hemingway and been in awe of the book, can be seen in another letter to Hortense Flexner dated on August twenty-fifth, 1940:

*'Meantime Scrooby's book is nearly finished: that is to say really finished, as Scribner's set it up in type the minute they got their*

*hands on it. We have been reading and correcting galleys and as it is about 200,000 words long that is no joke for anyone. But it is very fine indeed, oh my what a book. It is all alive, all exciting, all true, and with many discoveries about life and living and death and dying: which in the end is all there is to write about. I am proud of it and so is Scrooby and maybe we can rest easy for a bit.'[24]*

Life and death are topics that are to be found in Hemingway's very earliest stories which stretch back to long before his war experiences – even back to his college days and to his times in Michigan where he was influenced by the natural world and stories relating to it. Conversely, life in Chicago is rarely reflected in Hemingway's work.

In his novel, *To Whom the Bell Tolls*, there is, however, a passage referring to the experience Ernest had, as a seventeen year old, of being dropped at the train station by his father when on his way to Kansas. In the book, the protagonist, Robert Jordan, had felt more insecure than he'd felt for a long time just as he was about to step into the train at Red Lodge on his way to school at Billings. Hemingway described it as follows:

'... *his father had kissed him good-by and said, "May the Lord watch between thee and me while we are absent the one from the other." His father had been a very religious man and he had said it simply and sincerely. But his moustache had been moist and his eyes were damp with emotion and Robert Jordan had been so embarrassed by all of it, the damp religious sound of the prayer, and by his father kissing him good-by, that he had suddenly felt so much older than his father and sorry for him that he could hardly bear it.'* [25]

Ernest would not, probably, have felt all that good being driven by his father to the station where he would take the train from there to Kansas before taking up his first job with *The Kansas Star*. It was an important newspaper at the time and was seen as one of the best in the Midwest of the United States. It was a good address to start with as the newspaper put emphasis on training young reporters.

His greatest influence at the paper was the assistant city editor, Pete Wellington, who Ernest worked directly under. Wellington wanted him to write in a short, crisp style. Here Hemingway worked hard, and was eager to make his way in the world. He was given a style sheet that outlined the 110 rules that young reporters were to follow in their writing:

*'Use short sentences. Use short first paragraphs. Use vigorous English. Be positive not negative. Eliminate every superfluous word. Dont split verbs. Avoid the use of adjectives, especially such extravagant ones as splendid gorgeous, grand, magnificent etc.'*[26]

Hemingway stayed with his uncle, Tyler, when he, first, came to Kansas, but a month later he moved in with his old friend, Carl Edgar, whom he had known from his summers in Michigan. Carl said of the fledging reporter:

*'Hemingway completely immersed himself in the charm and romance of working for a newspaper. He could talk for hours about his work, especially at times when it would have been better to go to bed.'*

He did write in short sentences and he wrote about things he experienced in and around Kansas City. On one occasion he ran through a crowd of curious bystanders to help a sick man at Union Station. When he saw the man really needed help, he carried him to a taxi and took him to hospital. This willingness to help, which would, later, earn him a medal of bravery when he was prepared to assist injured comrades even though he himself was severely wounded, had always been part of his personality. Hemingway always stepped in to support people in need and when he could, he would take care of them.

His stories range from a newspaper boy's fight to a sad story about a prostitute, to a shoot-out among gangsters; even to an article drawing attention to the everyday tragedies of a hospital Emergency Room. He had given up his job at the newspaper when he enlisted. On his return, much to the disapproval of his parents, especially his mother, he turned to writing. There is nothing unusual about family and community not approving of an emerging writer – and, sometimes, even when successful. Hemingway was conscious that he couldn't just write; he'd have to earn his living otherwise.

In October 1919, he paid a short visit to Chicago, but couldn't stand it and returned to Petoskey. He explained it by saying he wasn't able to write at home. In Petoskey he worked part-time at the local administration office to cover his basic needs as well as to take Marjorie out or to meet friends for a meal from time to time. But it wasn't always enough, so when the offer of a job in Toronto came up he was happy to move.

A rich family gave him a large room with a desk where he could work and, for this, he had to escort their handicapped son to theatre, concerts and sporting events. Thanks to the boy's father, he got a job with *The Toronto Star* which would take him back to Europe again – but only after his marriage to Hadley whom he hadn't met as yet. Examples of Hemingway's articles for *The Toronto Star*:

### Plain and Fancy Killings, $400 Up

*Gunman from the United State are being imported to do killings in Ireland. That is an established fact from Associated Press dispatches. According to the underworld gossip in New York and Chicago, every ship that leaves for England carries its one or two of these weasels of death bound for where the hunting is good. The underworld says that the gunmen are first shipped to England where there lose themselves in the waterfronts of cities like Liverpool and then slip over to Ireland.[27]*

### A free Shave

*The true home of the free and the brave is the barber college. Everything is free there. And you have to be brave. If you want to save $5.60 a month on shaves and haircuts, go to the barber but take your courage with you. For a visit to the barber college requires the cold, naked valor of the man who walks clear-eyed to death. If* *you don't believe it, go to the beginner's department of the barber's college and offer yourself for a free shave. I did.*[28]

His mother wrote a letter expressing her relative happiness at his success, but it still gnawed at her innards that her eldest son had not gone to college and *not* become a doctor which would have been fitting in a family that placed value on the status of qualification.

She was probably relieved that her son was now in a position to earn money with his writing. Nevertheless, it did not improve their relationship. Ernest, indeed, did return to his parent's house in Chicago in May 1920, but almost immediately left again for Horton Bay.

In July, he visited Windemere with two friends to celebrate his twenty-first birthday. His mother; she was, still, unable to accept that Ernest had made writing his profession and accused him of being unemployed. However, he was expected to be in Windemere in summer to take his father's place in his absence. The correspondence between his parents at the time tells that his mother, Grace, had complained about her son from day one.

Finally there was an inconsequential happening that concerned his sisters more than him. which led to him being thrown out of Windemere. Evidence would suggest it had been premeditated. His mother gave him a letter, that she must have written beforehand, because she would not have had time to have written such a detailed letter between the quarrel and the fact that he was thrown out. This letter displayed Grace's state of mind and the coldness she managed to generate – it is that the letter in which she compares a mother's love with a "bank account."

Afterwards and until the beginning of October, Ernest lived with Liz and Jim Dilworth. He supported himself by working for them and helping out here and there – otherwise he spent his time writing. It is said that Hemingway had his first sexual encounter with a woman during this time and that this experience is there to be read in his short story, *Up in Michigan*.

The story created ripples for other reasons: when Marceline, seen by their mother to be Ernest's twin, read the story, it almost "turned her stomach." Her disappointment did not derive from her brother's alleged first sexual experience, but from the fact that he had used the first names of the Dilworths, Liz and Jim, as his two participants in the encounter. The names of two recognizable, decent people, who were close friends of the Hemingway family.

In a letter, dated on August twelve, 1930 we see that Hemingway was, at least, conscious of the difficulty he had created:

*'Have gone over I.O.T. (In Our Time) also the Up In Michigan. I've rewritten it to try and keep it from being libelous but to do so takes all the character away. It clearly refers to two people in a given town, both of them still alive, still living there and easily identified. If I take the town away it loses veracity. But I can leave out enough of the first part to eliminate libel.'*

The reasons why the sex scenes are seen to be so closely bound up with him have, probably, to do with the fact that the first draft of the story, written in 1921, was written in the first person. Shortly afterwards, when reworking the story, he inserted the names, Liz and Jim – probably because he had married in the meantime. That first draft, which had initiated the autographical speculation, was drafted in summer 1921 in Chicago shortly before his wedding.

It is, however, difficult to understand why he'd used the names of good friends he'd always felt close to. Not only did he use their names but he also partly adopted their appearances and patterns of behavior. Today, it doesn't disturb Jim and Liz (as they, like Hemingway, are no longer with us) but for readers of *Up in Michigan*, the question remains: why did he do it? Was it intentional? The same question supplies a similar inconclusive answer when applied to the case of Prudy Boulton or Marjorie Bump. If Hemingway had not introduced an autographical element in the first draft of the story, the question, whether he's forced himself upon the young barmaid against her will, would, most likely, never have arisen.

Scholars, who have done detailed studies on Hemingway, are certain this incident took place at the bay down below Pinehurst Cottage at the end of Lake Street. They are also quite certain that he'd never had sex with his great love, Agnes von Kurowsky. This certainty is based on her farewell letter in which she says her feelings for him are more motherly than those of a sweetheart. They are just as sure that "nothing happened" in the case of Marjorie Bump or Prudy Boulton. According to the Nick Adams stories, these women would have come into question as "first time" candidates.

The short story, *Up in Michigan*, is not included in the *Nick Adams Stories*. It was, first, published in that little volume in Paris in 1923, that was already mentioned, with the title, *Three Stories and Ten Poems*. The good thing about being published in Paris meant that Liz and Jin Dilworth didn't get to see the story. On the twelve of January in 1936 Hemingway wrote a letter in which he stated that the story had not been published, but he'd forgotten the little Paris publication. But apart from that, *Up in Michigan*, was, indeed, published by Hemingway's publisher, Scribner as late as 1938.

The story was also removed from his short story collection, *In Our Time*, published in the USA in 1925. Hemingway was indignant about the fact. In a letter he wrote to John Dos Passos:

*'They made me take out the Up in Michigan story because the girl got yenced and I sent 'em a swell new Nick story... and better than Up in Michigan although I always liked Up in Mich although some did not. I supposed if it was called Way out in Iowa, Mencken would have published it if the fucking would have been changed to a community corn roast.'*

The story is simple and almost without plot. The smith, Jim, comes to Horton bay and purchases the local forge. The young woman, who works at Smith's restaurant, falls in love with Jim but he hardly notices her.

Jim, plus the restaurant owner, Smith, and a third person go on a hunting trip. Liz longs for Jim while he is away. When the hunting party returns, there are drinks to celebrate.

After dinner and a few more drinks, Jim goes into the kitchen where Liz is sitting on a chair. He embraces and kisses her, strokes her breasts and whispers, *come on for a walk,* whereupon they go down to the Bay.

Jim begins to stroke Liz's body. She is scared, repeats again and again that she doesn't want it, but she finally capitulates. The end of the story:

'*The hemlock planks of the dock were hard and splintery and cold and Jim was heavy on her and he had hurt her. Liz pushed him, she was so uncomfortable and camped. Jim was asleep. He wouldn't move. She worked out from under him and sat up and straightened her skirt and coat and tried to do something with her hair. Jim was sleeping with his mouth a little open. Liz leaned over and kissed him on the cheek. He was still asleep. She lifted his head a little and shook it. He rolled his head over and swallowed. Liz started to cry. She waled over to the edge of the dock and looked down to the water. There was a mist coming up from the bay. She was cold and miserable and everything felt gone. She walked back to where Jim was lying and shook him once more to make sure. She was crying.*

*"Jim," she said. "Jim. Please, Jim."*

*Jim stirred and curled a little tighter. Liz took off her coat and leaned over and covered him with it. She tucked it around him neatly and carefully. Then she walked across the dock and up the steep sandy road to go to bed. A cold mist was coming up through the woods from the bay.*

The story is crude and without feelings apart from those of the character of Liz. A young inexperienced woman is overcome by love for the older man, Jim, who is unable to satisfy her romantically or erotically. She kissed his cheek after he had mercilessly entered her body and, in the lifeless moments afterwards, she confessed her perpetual love for him and tried to get a reaction. When this reaction didn't come, she felt her life was over and she wept bitterly.

The one fascinating aspect of the story is that Hemingway tried to imagine he understood the fantasies of an inexperienced young woman and was capable to describe her conflicting emotions, even in the intense moments when they were coming to a brutal and savage end. How he manages, in a few words, to expose the injured soul of a young woman; how he suggests that Liz understood Jim only wanted her for his sexual gratification and how he describes the emptiness and feelings of hopelessness when it is over... All of it points to the emergence of the outstanding writer he was to become.

Much later in 1936, Hemingway expresses an opinion, worthy of note, at the end of the story:

*'It is an important story in my work and one that has influenced many people. Callaghan etc. It is not dirty but is very sad. I did not write so well then, especially dialogues. Much of the dialogue is very wooden in that story. But there on the dock it suddenly got absolutely right and it is the point of the whole story and the beginning of all the naturalness I ever got.'*

This statement is in no way helpful when it comes to the question as to whether it was Ernest who had had sex down there on the planks of the dock. The formulations do not lend us clues and otherwise there is little to suggest that he had. One could imagine Ernest's first encounter with an unwilling and inexperienced young woman, but to say that the story is autobiographical is improbable seeing as Jim was an experienced man. From what is known of Hemingway and his character, this would not have been consistent with his behavior.

Most probably the first sexual encounter he would have had with a woman would have been with his wife, Hadley. There is no evidence to suggest that he'd been with women of openly seductive behavior. Hemingway was 22 years old when he married and, from the standpoint of nowadays, this would have been late, but a century ago it wasn't unusual. This could be an opinion before one discovers the letter Hemingway had written to Bill Horne after Agnes von Kurowsky had rejected him. Hemingway lamented having left her: *'She needs somebody to make love to her. If the right person turns up, you're out of luck.'*

At this stage, one can assume that Hemingway had a sexual relationship with Agnes and, it would seem as if she was the first woman he'd slept with.

What makes *Up in Michigan* special is neither if Hemingway was the man who takes advantage of a young barmaid nor if it is his first experience of sex – much more important is the literary perspective of Hemingway, the storyteller. At the end of the story it is the point of view of the woman and her experiences that is central to his writing.

A young man who has allegedly become what others, including his mother, suppose him to be: a young waster without any sense of responsibility who spent his time fishing and hunting, who had little or no interest in his education, and who hung about with mates drinking more than he should. You'd imagine that such a man, when writing a story, would be attracted to write from the point of view of the violent seducer and not from the perspective of a sensitive, injured young woman. Hemingway was different. His interest was not only in the ruthless, hormone-driven man, but more in the inexperience, feelings, needs and dreams of the woman. He had a sympathetic and caring nature, otherwise he could not have written about such matters. A writer writes what he deeply feels about. We come across this sympathetic nature again in his dealings with his sister in *The Last Good Country* and with Marjorie in *The End of Something*.

Owning up to being sympathetic or admitting to tenderness and sensitivity was not really what his writing was about. More than likely, these feelings were to be concealed in his every day life. Concessions to tenderness and emotional weakness would have taken him to an area he, most certainly, did not want to open himself. He'd have to appear unmanly and submit himself to the influence of his mother – to be weak and delivered up to her overwhelming domination as his father had been.

From Hemingway's childhood and youth spent fishing and hunting, it can be seen that exposure to the rawness of nature does not necessarily cloak sensibility of character – on the contrary it strengthens it. This is supported by his intense longing for and love of the natural world. He loved just being there and he enjoyed fishing above all else. He adored the long summers and would feel quite ill in the first weeks in August when he realized the trout-fishing season would be coming to an end in about four weeks. He would worship the looming storms when he'd have to cross the lake by a boat with his shopping and his post. He'd have to sit on his newspaper to protect it from the rain and, afterwards, have to dry his clothes in front of the open fire, as a biographer wrote. This was an incomparable pleasure for him.

After his marriage, apart from short visits, Hemingway seemed to turn his back on Michigan. At first glance this looks to be a contradiction in terms but, in fact, all he'd wanted was to re-member his Paradise as he had known it; wanted to keep his love for it alive as it had been in its original state. He was probably aware that in his new life there would be no place for the casual love affair he'd conducted with his Michigan.

This Michigan had meant so much to him. It was about the only place or thing that helped to alleviate and lessen the memory of war. It was here in Michigan that he'd sensed the need to put pen to paper for the first time. The background to some of his last ex-periences there – his fishing trips to the Upper Peninsula – comes to life in *The Big Two-Hearted River*.

Travelling to Michigan's Upper Peninsula by car on the way to St. Ignace, you cross a suspension bridge where Lake Huron and Lake Michigan meet. Hemingway travelled by train in those days. At this time, he had not, yet, crossed the beautiful Mackinac Bridge – the third longest bridge in the world nowadays. It was first open to traffic in 1957.

In Hemingway days, one still crossed the lakes by ferry. From St. Ignace to Seney was 180 kilometers. However, the "Big Two Hearted River", which gave the story its name, does not flow to

Seney. As a matter of fact it is about 50 kilometers away from this Place. Hence, those wishing to trace the movements of Hemingway can save themselves a trip to "Big Two Hearted River". Hemingway gave the story this name because, in his opinion, the name of this river sounded more impressive than "Fox River" where the story is, in fact, located. As well as this, this River does flow through the place that is mentioned with a railway line. The character, Nick Adams arrives there by train and heads immediately for the river.

For the story, the name of the river is relatively unimportant, as indeed are the geographical names – even if, because of the story, one of them managed to achieve world fame and the other one does not. Those in charge in the district were proud to have their "Big Two Hearted River" receive reference in a Hemingway story – a plaque on the riverbank stated: '*The Mighty Two Hearted River immortalized by Ernest Hemingway.*'[29] Sadly, the plaque was not immortal because it no longer exists.

*The Big Two Hearted River*! What a wonderful name! One has to agree with Hemingway: it is far more lyrical than Fox River. The name is Indian in its origin and means twin or double river, which also points to the fact that there were two rivers close together, both flowing into Lake Superior. The word, heart, in the name was apparently inserted by settlers. The river, embedded in a placid landscape, bends and curves its way through a colorful landscape and does not convey the feeling that, here, we are dealing with a stream, or a great river with two hearts. In reality, there is one small river next to an even smaller one. Perhaps Ojibwa-Indians could have enlightened us on the significance of the *heart* in the name – they called it *Neeshoda Sepee* – or perhaps the first white settlers could have thrown light on the subject.

But the real meaning in Hemingway's story is teased out by the reader. It has to do with longing – a yearning for things as they used to be. The world can stay on the outside and the character of Nick Adams – in whom Hemingway is easily identifiable – would like his future life to be lived out undisturbed and in harmony with the nature he loves so much.

He is a returnee, who has suffered from the Great War in Europe. Wounded, he reaches the town of Seney, which in the story has, like the surrounding forests and countryside, been burned to the ground. He walks away from it as he did from the war.

He was back to nature, to a scorched landscape and a burned out soul. Destroyed. Nature destroyed by fire and a soul destroyed by war. Today we talk of "burnout" and label intense mental trauma or suffering as Post Traumatic Stress. The atmosphere and mood of the story is conveyed in the following excerpt:

*'As he smoked, his legs stretched out in front of him, he noticed a grasshopper walk along the ground and up onto his woolen socks. The grasshopper was black. As he walked along the road, climbing, he had started many grasshoppers from the dust. They were all black. They were not the big grasshoppers with yellow and black or red and black wings whirring out from their black wing sheathing as they fly up. These were just ordinary hoppers, but all a sooty black in color. Nick had wondered about them as he walked, without really thinking about them. Now, as he watched that black hopper that was nibbling at the wool of his socks with its four-way lip, he realized that they had all turned black from living in the burned-over land. He wondered how long they would stay that way.*

*Carefully he reached his hand down and took hold of the hopper by the wings. He turned him up, all his legs walking in the air, and looked at his jointed belly. Yes, it was black too, iridescent where the back and head were dusty.*

*"Go on, hopper," Nick said, speaking out loud for the first time. "Fly away somewhere."*

The black grasshopper marks a return from war – it symbolizes Nick's state of mind and soul in the story. It's a sign of conflagration where everything is burned except for the river and it's the river that provides him with relief and happiness. When he jumped from the train at Seney, he'd expected an intact town, but when he saw the destruction, he did a quick turnabout and headed for the bridge without his luggage.

*The river was there.*'

Of course the river was still there, but for Nick it was more a statement of relief, almost as if when in a discourse on Hemingway, the river could be seen to possess healing powers for his broken heart. Hemingway, who had been severely wounded wrote in an unpublished manuscript:

'*And every July they took him out and broke his heart.* '[30]

In this manuscript, the narrator tells of a wounded young man whose heart has been broken by his experiences of war. His words, to the black grasshopper, *go on hopper,* as he sets it free, represents his own wish to escape destruction, but the hopper only flies to the next blackened stump.

There is no escape. The anxiety is permanent. The only hope of salvation lies in the question: how long a grasshopper would remain black? A bit like the river with its intact system and promises of magnificent trout.

Ernest Hemingway was twenty-five years old at the time of writing the story and this was six years after he'd been severely wounded in an exchange of fire in The First World War. At that time, in the United States and elsewhere, it was taken for granted that it was the duty of every patriotic young man to serve his country in time of war. But it wasn't only the *Zeitgeist* that drove Ernest into the army before he'd reached the appropriate age. How could a young man better express himself as a real man and not as a coward like his father? The father's attitude and lack of understanding of Ernest had been problematic since adolescence of his son, but more problematic still had been his father's total subordination to his wife who, in the eyes of Ernest, had degraded her husband and his father to the role of a "coward.".

Ernest's emotional connection to his mother and feelings for her were not even close to that love that he had for his father. This had to do with the fact that the son held his mother responsible for his father's behavior. In Ernest's eyes she was the one who stood in the way of his wish to have a proper relationship with his father; thus preventing the growth of a truly fatherly element in the family. From his early years Ernest felt alone with these feelings. He said to himself he could never be weak or cowardly – he might end up like his father. He might not have had a clear definition of how a man should be, but of one thing he was certain: never to become like his father.

Ernest was just 19 years old when he was confronted with the horrendous realities of war, when he began to realize that "not being a coward" could cost a life, and when real bodily pain and suffering was inflicted upon him. He ached to return to the life that for him was the life of a proper man: to be back among the forests, the dunes, plantations, lakes and rivers of Michigan. He longed to be at peace and in harmony with himself and his world. He yearned to fish, hunt, and be alone with himself and his books and above all, to be in touch with the two things that made up the essence of life as he saw it: nature and literature.

In the story, *The Big Two Hearted River*, Hemingway, as the character of Nick, gives us some insight as to why he chose to return to a landscape ravaged by fire. For him it probably had symbolic character: a scorched landscape that had lost its innocence to fire and a broken young man, who had lost his carefree past to war, had a lot in common. The burned out and deserted land evoked feelings of destruction of which he'd just had first-hand experience. The new freedom, he yearned for, could only be reborn and revitalized out of the ashes of destruction and despair. His return to the world of nature would have been a return to the past that no longer existed – to the Paradise he had lost.

But there was hope of relief in the symbol of the "grasshopper:" Hemingway's *alter ego* Nick asks himself how long it would remain black. The question suggests that the effects of a catastrophe do not remain forever.

Further into the story, Nick is overcome by feelings of contentment. He can decide what he wants to eat; where he'll sleep and despite strenuous trekking, he is happy to be able to decide where and when he wants to go next. As can be seen in one of the story's passages, his happiness is almost complete, except for one, typically Hemingwean wish – a book:

*'He spread the mouth of the sack and looked down in at the two big trout alive in the water. Through the deepening water, Nick waded over to the hollow log. He took the sack off, over his head, the trout flopping as it came out of water, and hung it so the trout were deep in the water. Then he pulled himself up on the log and sat, the water from his trousers and boots running down into the stream. He laid his rod down, moved along to the shady end of the log and took the sandwiches out of his pocket. He dipped the sandwiches in the cold water. The current carried away the crumbs. He ate the sandwiches and dipped his hat full of water to drink, the water running out through his hat just ahead of his drinking.*

*It was cool in the shade, sitting on the log. He took a cigarette out and struck a match to light it. The match sunk into the gray wood, making a tiny furrow. Nick leaned over the side of the log, find a hard place and lit the match. He sat smoking and watching the river…*

*He wished he had brought something to read. He felt like reading. He did not feel like going on into the swamp. He looked down the river. A big cedar slanted all the way across the stream. Beyond that the river went into the swamp.'*

In his writing in the *Nick Adams Stories*, we find out why Hemingway wrote so much about Michigan compared to what he'd written about Oak Park, Chicago, although he had spent a lot more time there. Also, in his other works, there is little Oak Park influence, but lots of Michigan. Why? The answer is simple and easily deduced from that passage in the *Nick Adams Stories*: he loved nature and because he only wanted to write about things that touched his heart, about things that he could feel strongly and artfully express in words.

In his writing, every author would only try to translate images as he or she sees them. All of these perceived descriptions are present in all of us but it is the writer's desire and energy that breathes flesh into the bones of a picture. If his impressions of Oak Park did not evoke pictures in the mind of the young Ernest, he'd probably have nothing to write about. There are opinions and voices that suggest that he didn't choose to write about his time in Oak Park because he would have been obliged to write about friends of the family and their surroundings. There would almost certainly have been negative spin-off which might have scared him off.

The hidden symbolism which is constantly attributed to Hemingway's work can be traced back to his own explanation of what writing should be. Important for him, is not only what's on the page in a story, but what's not or is hidden between the lines.

It is also worth noting that, for him, there is a great difference between something not displayed and something that is displayed or obvious in writing. It could be that the writer is not fully in charge of his subject matter and, as a consequence, leaves something out or, conversely, the good writer, deliberately, leaves it out to make a difference. In his own words:

*'A few things I have found to be true. If you leave out important things or events that you know about, the story is strengthened. If you leave or skip something because you do not know it, the story will be worthless. The test of every story is how very good the stuff is that you, not your editors, omit.'*

Hemingway said that just because you can write short stories does not mean you are obliged to explain them. And if a person cannot write, no amount of explanation will help. In other words the readers should be free to use their imagination when reading what's on the page or what's hidden between the lines. However, Hemingway did make an exception and added a short explanation to the "Big Hearted River" story:

*A story in this book called "Big Two-Hearted River" is about a boy coming home beat to the wide from a war. Beat to the wide was an earlier and possibly more severe form of beat, since those who had it were unable to comment on this condition and could not suffer that it be mentioned in their presence. So the war, all mention of the war, anything about the war, is omitted. The river was the Fox River, by Seney, Michigan, not the Big Two-Hearted. The change of name was made purposely, not from ignorance nor carelessness but because Big Two-Hearted River is poetry, and because there were many Indians nor the war appeared. As you see, it is very simple and easy to explain.'*

At the beginning, critics had great difficulty with the story. Perhaps they were not in tune with the author's background. The story was first published in Paris by Ernest Walsh and Ethel Moorehead in their Journal, *This Quarter*, in 1925. Nothing happens in the story. Hemingway wrote, exclusively, about a fishing trip. But it is this fishing trip that helped the returning soldier to heal and forget the wounds that war had inflicted on his body and soul – and here he is not referring to the wounds in character's Nick leg. Hemingway's *alter ego* is relieved and happy to be back in Seney. This is one pointer to the depth of the story which gradually began to reveal itself to critics.

Today the symbolic elements in the story tend to outweigh all others. For example, the American author and literary critic, Malcolm Cowley, sees the fishing trip:

*'...as a flight from a nightmare to reality, or from realities that have become nightmare worlds.'*

Seney is a little place on Highway 28 and is, probably, not much bigger than it was hundred years ago. In Hemingway's own description, the highway crosses the Fox River a little north of the railroad tracks. The bridge across the river is the bridge from where he stood looking into the river and from where he could see trouts. It is the bridge in Railroad Street. From the bridge, Nick Adams saw clear water gone slightly brown from the stony river bed, and he saw trouts holding themselves still in the current *by tiny movements of their fins.*

Hemingway went to Seney and surrounding areas to fish in summer of 1919 and in the late summer of 1920. He talked of the forthcoming 1920 journey in a letter dated on August the first of that year:

*In Seney in a few weeks.*

In fact, he was not met by a scorched landscape, but it is confirmed that in the year 1891, Seney was completely destroyed by fire and, again in 1895 when the restored town was partially destroyed again. Therefore it is probable that Hemingway chose a burned out town and a scorched landscape for reasons already mentioned. The story was written in 1924. From a literary perspective this is interesting, because it was a time when Hemingway was trying to change his style from that of a reporter to that of an author and a novelist.

Gertrude Stein – the American writer of novels, poetry and plays who made Paris her home – was the one who had encouraged him to change. She was of the opinion that journalism and literature were, as writing forms, diametrically opposed. The journalist is more inclined *to inform or report than to create*, and she believed it is better *to create than to merely inform or report.*

Hemingway placed great value on the opinion and instruction of Gertrude Stein. When one compares his texts on his experiences of fishing in an article from *The Toronto Star*, written in 1920, with his short story *The Big Two-Hearted River* on the same subject, it shows how carefully he had followed her instructions. In a discussion with her in 1924, he confirmed how "easy" writing, in this way, had become since meeting her. He had got to know her two months after his marriage to Hadley and just before he was being sent to Paris as a foreign correspondent for *The Toronto Star.*

In Hemingway's eyes Stein was involved, stylistically at least, in *The Big Two-Hearted River* story. The reasons why this story and its symbolism are not totally bound up with his war experiences have to do with the fact that, as well as his war trauma in the years 1919 and 1920, he was grappling with his problematic relationship with his mother – that reached its sad climax in 1920 when she threw him out of Windemere then. Furthermore, Agnes, his great love from his time in the field-hospital in Italy, had sent him that letter rejecting his declaration of love.

The biographer, Kenneth S. Lynn is of the opinion that the metaphor in the *Big Two-Hearted River* story has to do, exclusively, with the mother-son's conflict. Lynn bases this assumption on the feelings of happiness that Nick experiences when he builds his tent, because he sees his tent as a home he has created for himself: *He was in his home where he had made it.*

*The Big Two-Hearted River* story was written four or five years after his fishing trip to Seney. It would appear that, as well as his war scars, the trip might have awakened other scars. They had to do with the memory of being thrown out of his parent's home and the complicated, lifelong relationship he'd had with his mother. It is imaginable that the homely tent, where he could cuddle up in his sleeping bag, had been a special home for Hemingway. It is possible to draw such conclusions when one reads that he had left all essential needs behind him and could rejoice in his independence, and freedom to pursue the activity he loved most of all: fishing in one of the most beautiful creeks in Michigan.

The fact that his writing was inspired only by his ongoing disputes with his mother and the fact that she "showed him the door" in 1920, are doubtful – he did not go camping directly afterwards. As well as this, his expulsion took place in 1920 – his big fishing trip to Seney in 1919 which was repeated in late-summer 1920 – but he had lived alone for quite a while in Horton Bay after his mother asked him to leave. It would appear as if he had not embarked on a great fishing trip because he had nothing better to do. Lynn's theory doesn't seem to have much going for it. It suggests, Hemingway thought of his home situation and what Nick had left behind him. For example, he needed time to think, to write and do some other things that needed to be done. Lynn's reasoning is too weak to be accepted. His main argument, that the war experiences were not significant, is based on the fact that the story does not discuss the war. He held on to his opinion even though Hemingway, himself, had said that he'd deliberately omitted the war descriptions while stating that the story is about a boy coming home from war: *So the war, all mention of the war, anything about the war, is omitted.*[31]

This explanation, published after Hemingway's death, left the biographer, Lynn, no option other than to suggest that these words of Hemingway – *the master of manipulation even from the grave* – could be considered as reviewers' cliché. He based this opinion on the fact that Hemingway had said nothing about the subject over such a long period.[32]

One can't condemn Kenneth S. Lynn for having had his own theory, but what he can be criticized for, is that he considers his theory, alone, as being valid. That Hemingway did not write the truth about suffering in war is, perhaps, true. It was his, Hemingway's, opinion that all writers were liars –including him, of course.

In the light of his firm adherence to his theory, Kenneth S. Lynn could be described as a scholar who would always have considered his theory to be absolute and correct even when a few spoke in its favor. He would also have believed that Hadley, Hemingway's first wife, is the woman referred to in *The End of Something*, although it is clear from a Hemingway letter that she is not. Throughout his life, Hemingway had been a storyteller who'd often mixed up truth and fiction – the fact that, in itself, proves nothing. He'd always said The First World War had taken away from him a lot of sleep, but he'd owed it to himself, as a *man*, to overcome his insomnia by his own power. According to Hemingway himself, he was in perfect condition. This is to be found in Lynn's biography. He also set up a connection between Hemingway's war experiences and poor physical and mental state, judging from Hemingway's words: *refused to get medical assistance…* And by this he meant Hemingway's poor condition since the late nineteen forties. Further to this, Lynn added: *From Hemingway's poor condition, it is obvious to anyone that he is boasting and talking himself up when he claims he has overcome his insomnia.*

Here, in this context, the biographer would claim his statement to be true, which in another context he would have depicted as deception.

It is now recognized that traumatic experiences, such as post-traumatic stress, can last a lifetime. It is also acknowledged, it can take years – even decades in some cases – for the sufferer to be in a position to face up this condition.

Even from a storyteller like Hemingway, we must take seriously his letter to Malcolm Cowley dated on August the twenty-fifth, 1948, where he stated that he, all in all, was badly injured in war and a nervous wreck at the end of it.

Post-traumatic stress disorder (PTSD) is a relatively new phenomenon. It was first recognized as a consequence of war after the war in Vietnam, and it was the war veterans who were first to define it as suffering and an illness, and who saw to it that it was included in the official handbook of psychological disturbances in the year 1980. This, of course, did not change the perception of the population at large that would have branded these veterans as weaklings – how much more must this have been the case in earlier wars. Since, that this effect first appeared and was taken seriously in the eighties does not mean that it had not been present in the past.

Ernest Hemingway's drinking problem before the war may have been an indication of his predestination to become an alcoholic. He'd begun drinking as a youth – to be precise, since he was fifteen. He even admitted hardly anything gave him more pleasure. That young people enjoy alcohol and, sometimes, drink to excess is nothing new. Nevertheless, drinking like this in younger years is not the only indication of later addiction. There could be underlying factors that awaken the disposition and evoke dependency. A connection between post-traumatic stress and alcohol addiction is something that cannot easily be ignored or contradicted, but one can never really know if Hemingway's family difficulties alone were at the root of his addiction. Then even before his nineteenth birthday, Ernest Hemingway's life took a decisive turn, which could be seen to have influenced or been the cause of his behavior in later years. However, his childhood upbringing and his experience of war as a young man present occasion enough for later addiction.

His time in Europe in The First World War, and especially the physical wounds he received, were basis for another form of injury he'd been inflicted with: the injury to his heart that his love of Agnes von Kurowsky had caused. This is which had never got a chance to blossom and remained unanswered. Agnes literally didn't acknowledge him "as a man". His love remained unfulfilled and he fell into the depths of depression. The residue of this experience stayed with him for many years.

His novel, *The Sun Also Rises*, published in 1926 in Paris, gives us an account of Hemingway's time in writing circles in that city in the nineteen twenties, and in Spanish Pamplona in 1924. There is the account of a scene where the first person narrator, the author Jacob Barnes, suffers serious injury on the Italian front during The First World War. He gets to know the nurse Brett and falls in love with her. In his book, *A Farewell to Arms*, published three years later, he, again, taps into his experience of his unrequired love. The protagonist in the story, Frederic Henry, has, in general, respect for war but, he himself, has no intention of dying in the battle: *Not in war. It has nothing to do with me.* Henry's world is simple. He concerns himself little with the war.

Passini, another character in the novel, is the exact opposite. He protests vehemently against the war; wants to see it end; hopes the Austrians will get tired and disappear. Passini is killed in a hand grenade attack and Henry is injured. Henry is visited in hospital by a priest who presents him with a medal of bravery. In real life, the priest is Don Guiseppe Bianci who became friends with Ernest during his stay in Italy. In the novel, Henry is transferred to a hospital in Milan, exactly as it was in Ernest's real life, as well as here he falls in love with the nurse, Catherine, and she responds to his love. Despite Frederic's injury, they make love during her night duty. Catherine becomes pregnant. On Frederic's release from hospital, they spend a few hours in a comfortable hotel in Milan. Afterwards, Frederic had to return to his regiment and becomes involved in war negotiations which result in a chaotic mess. He gets into civilian clothes and meets Catherine at Lake Maggiore, but must be careful not to be arrested as deserter. So he flees across the lake with her into Switzerland. Catherine wants to get married after they settle. There are complications during the birth of their child. A boy is born, but, it is tragic – Catherine dies of internal bleeding.

This love story is described in a direct but, at the same time, lyrical language. Hemingway's third wife, Martha Gellhorn, whom he had not known personally at this time, rejected him in the beginning but after reading the book, changed her mind. Hemingway and Gellhorn met for the first time on Christmas in 1936. While visiting Key West, Florida, with her mother and brother, she met Hemingway one evening at a bar by name of "Sloppy Joe's". There he sat:

*A large, dirty man in untidy somewhat soiled white shorts and shirt.*[33]

Thus she met the man whom she had written about in a letter in summer 1930 the following words:

*On the other hand I think Hemingway is pretty bum from what he did in* "In Our Time": *the story about skiing is written about an ex-beau of mine who used to ski with him. Hemingway makes him inarticulate simply because Hemingway doesn't know how to talk, as a matter of fact that guy can talk in 9 syllable words all night long. So I'm not impressed. Anyway Hemingway has affected my style which is really too bad; but there you are.* [34]

In the novel, *A farewell to Arms*, she was accosted by feelings she would not have attributed to Hemingway. In May 1931, she wrote to her former English teacher, Stanley Pennell at the John Burrows School (he would make a name for himself later):

*Meantime, I take my code out of Hemingway. Unbelievable, isn't? Do you remember A Farewell to Arms. The hero talks to the woman; she is worried about something; and she sais: 'You're brave. Nothing ever happens to the brave'. Which is somehow enough – a whole philosophy – a banner – a song – and love.* [35]

As was often the case with Hemingway, this apparently powerful masculine guy could convince by demonstration of his feelings in a tight, precise writing style, that is all the more impressive because of this very style. There were periods in real life when he lived out the bawdy hero type, but at the same time his work gives us flashes of insights into his sensitive soul.

His love for Agnes, the nurse, might have seemed unusual as she was eight years his senior but, then again, his first wife, Hadley, was also eight years older than him which, in turn, might lead one to conclude that this had something to do with the complicated relationship he shared with his mother.

Towards the end of 1920, Hemingway moved back living in Chicago, albeit not with his parents. Here, through their mutual friend, Katy Smith, he got to know Hadley Richardson from St. Louis. Katy, that future wife of John de Passos, had invited Hadley to Chicago to console and comfort her somewhat after the death of her mother who had passed away some time previously. Hemingway, now writing stories for *The Toronto Star*, fell in love with her and, very soon, it became clear that they would marry – even if he did have his doubts about getting married after such a short time of being out of love. He confidentially informed his friend Bill Smith in a letter where he wrote that he was going slightly mad with the thought that he would no longer be able to go to Michigan on those fishing trips that he'd always gone on "as on a loose foot" and fancy being free bachelor.

Michigan was his paradise. It was the place he chose to celebrate his marriage to his first wife. That he never returned there, in the same way, had to do with the break and change of life direction his marriage had made. All the happenings and experiences that had turned Michigan into his Garden of Eden were no longer part of his life – he wanted to keep them safe and undisturbed for himself in his memory. When he did return for the first time in 1940, he had the following to say:

*I've always been disappointed in places where I've returned. I have such loving memories of northern Michigan that I didn't want them interrupted.*[36]

If, at the beginning, the young Ernest had his doubts and was missing his fishing trips with his friends, his love grew stronger and got compensated for. At their first meeting in Chicago, not only was Hadley struck by Ernest's good looks: *he was so attractive,* but he was also carried away by her. This is what Hadley said:

*Ernest told someone years later that when I came into the room and was standing in the doorway, he knew that I was the girl he is going to marry.*[37]

It is interesting that he chose Horton Bay in Michigan for the wedding reception and not Oak Park, Chicago. This had little or nothing to do with the tension within the Hemingway's family – but more with his attraction to the area around Horton Bay.

He felt it to be a good time as there wouldn't be many people in the area around Horton Bay at the beginning of September. He could celebrate his wedding with people he really wanted to have around him.

Even if the purpose of his return was to celebrate his wedding, he wouldn't have been Ernest Hemingway, if he didn't take the opportunity to embark on a fishing trip. He arrived at Walloon Lake on August twenty-eight and immediately set out on a three-day fishing trip to the nearby Sturgeon River.

For the wedding he invited all of his friends and his family made the event into what was, probably, the biggest occasion that Horton Bay had ever experienced. Not present was his sister Marceline. Although she wrote about the wedding at a later stage, but Ursula commented on the inaccuracies in the text:

*Marceline couldn't give an accurate description of Ernest's wedding to Hadley, because she wasn't there. Carol, Leicester and I where the only brother and sisters there.[38]*

The wedding could have taken place in Hadley's home town, St. Louis. A local newspaper had already written about it, but Hemingway would have none of it – he even joked about bringing people to the backwoods. In a letter on his twenty-second birthday, he wrote:

*... but we're going to fool them and be married at the Bay in that small, trick church there.*

The honeymoon was spent in Windemere. Hemingway refers to it in the story, *Wedding Day*. John Kotesky, a local resident, drove the couple down to the lake in his car. Hemingway wrote:

*Nick paid John Kotesky five dollars and Kotesky helped him carry the bags down to the rowboat. They both shook hands with Kotesky and then his Ford went back up along the road. They could hear it for a long time...*

*It was a long row across the lake in the dark. The night was hot and depressing. Neither of them talked much. A few people had spoiled the wedding. Nick rowed hard when they were near shore and shot the boat up on the sandy beach. He pulled it up and Helen stepped out. Nick kissed her. She kissed him back hard the way he had taught her with her mouth a little open so their tongues could play with each other. They held tight to each other and then walked up to the cottage. It was dark and long. Nick unlocked the door and then went back to the boat to get the bags. He lit the lamps and they looked through the cottage together.*

This might appear to have been romantic, but the honeymoon was on shaky ground. The weather was terrible and both caught a cold. On a trip to Petoskey, Hemingway decided to introduce his new bride to friends – among them was Marjorie which did not went well with Hadley. After two weeks the young couple were happy to leave their holiday home and return to Chicago.

The "tiny toy church" is, sadly to say, no longer in Horton Bay but otherwise the place is not unlike it was at the time when the young writer lived, loved and married here. Most of the houses along the road from Boyne City to Charlevoix, described in his stories are still there.

The street is not so heavily frequented and it is easy to imagine Hemingway travelling on it with one of his sisters or with his friend, Bill Smith – going to the General Store to buy something, or simply sitting on the verandah in front of it. One could imagine him going to the Fox Inn, one house farther, to collect his friend, Vollie Fox for a day's fishing, or going diagonally across, and down the Lake Street to Jim and Liz Dilworth at Pinehurst Cottage. He can also been imagined down at the Lake Street pier, settled down with a fishing rod as he used to do.

We can immersing ourselves fully in this magical countryside and finding us faraway in long-ago time that is named in *The Nick Adams Stories*. There captured in the immortal sentences of a young man hungry for life and full of ambition to become one of America's most influential writers of the twentieth century.

# Notes

[1] Dr. Constance Cappel, *Hemingway in Michigan*, p. 10

[2] Robert W. Lewis, *Hemingway in Italy, Journal of Modern Literature*, May 1982, p. 223-24

[3] Georgianna Main, *Pip Pip to Hemingway in Something from Marge*, p. 9

[4] Larry W. Phillips (ed.), *Ernest Hemingway on Writing*, p. 11

[5] Ernest Hemingway, *The Nick Adams Stories*, (*Preface* by Philip Young) p. 5

[6] Dr. Constance Cappel, *Hemingway in Michigan*, p. 60

[7] ibid., p. 62

[8] *Georgianna Main, Pip Pip to Hemingway in Something from Marge*, p. 14

[9] ibid.

[10] H. R. Stoneback, *Nothing what ever Lost, Hemingway – Up in Michigan Perspectives*, p. 59

[11] *Georgianna Main, Pip Pip to Hemingway in Something from Marge*, p. 6

[12] H. R. Stoneback, *Hemingway – Up in Michigan Perspectives* p. 63

[13] Villard and Nagel, *Hemingway in Love and War*, p. 202

[14] Ian Maloney, *Ernest Hemingway's Miltonic Twist in "Up in Michigan"*

[15] Kenneth S. Lynn, *Hemingway*, p. 55

[16] Bernice Kert, *The Hemingway Woman*, New York 1983., p. 21.

[17] Kenneth S. Lynn, *Hemingway*, p. 133

[18] ibid., p. 51

[19] Peter Griffin, *Along with Youth*, p. 113-4

[20] ibid., p. 122

[21] Dr. Constance Cappel, *Hemingway in Michigan*, p. 147

[22] Caroline Moorhead, *Selected Letters from Martha Gellhorn*, p. 106

[23] ibid., p. 90

[24] ibid., p. 99

[25] Francis McGovern, *The Lessons of Youth: Ernest Hemingway as a Young Man*

[26] ibid.

[27] *The Toronto Star Weekly*, 11 December 1920

[28] *ibid.*, 6 March 1920

[29] Tina Lonski, *A Transplanted Yooper*, p. 25

[30] Frederic J. Svoboda and Joseph J. Waldmeir, *Hemingway, Up in Michigan Perspectives*, p. 78

[31] Jackson J. Benson, *New critical approaches to the short stories of Ernest Hemingway*, p. 3

[32] Kenneth S. Lynch, Hemingway, p. 131

[33] Caroline Moorhead, Selected *Letters from Martha Gellhorn*, p. 45

[34] ibid., p. 8

[35] ibid., p. 11

[36] James Barron, *Up in Michigan*, 24. November 1985

[37] Dr. Constance Cappel, *Hemingway in Michigan*, p. 177

[38] ibid., p. 175

18402451R00069

Made in the USA
Middletown, DE
05 March 2015